Paul McDowell was born and raised in London. In his present incarnation he has, at some time or other, been a painter, a pop singer, an actor, a plasterer's mate and a bongo player.

He is a student of Lee Chuan Fa Chinese Boxing, but nowhere near as accomplished in the art as Stan Garland.

Paul McDowell

Dope Opera

Pluto Press

First published in 1987 by Pluto Press
11–21 Northdown St., London N1 9BN

Typeset by AKM Associates (UK) Limited,
Ajmal House, Hayes Road, Southall, London
Printed in Great Britain by Cox & Wyman Limited,
Reading, Berks.

British Library Cataloguing in Publication Data
McDowell, Paul
    Dope opera —— (Pluto crime)
    I. Title
    823′.914[F]   PR6063.A178/

    ISBN 0 7453 0119 3 pbk
         0 7453 0124 X hbk

One

They didn't look like trouble. True, the one with 'Mick' spelled out in metal studs over the back of his black leather jacket had a nasty look about him. But the jacket hung loosely over a skinny, wasted, bony frame you could have struck red-topped matches on. His Mohican haircut was dyed a patchy purple colour, and it was surrounded by a rash of tiny shaving nicks. Seen up close, some of the nicks were clearly turning septic – an effect that could have been intentional. Mick was a sometime performance artist. The division between life and performance art tends to blur easily. At least it does to my prejudiced eye.

'Dave' was picked out in rusting studs, and the jacket was stretched tight over folds and wads of soft flesh. Dave couldn't have been more than twenty-five, but his jawline was gone, and there was an old man's beer paunch hanging over his jeans. The jeans rested upon a pair of Cuban-heeled boots that brought Dave up to five six, or possibly seven.

He and Mick didn't look like trouble. But you can't always tell. That was why the right-hand pocket of my raincoat held a short length of iron bar.

Dave, pint glass of beer in hand, turned to rest his elbows on the counter behind. His face was flushed and sweaty, and his eyes were having trouble in focusing. Letting rip with a loud belch, Dave flicked aside a long strand of dirty blond hair and raised the beer glass to his mouth. When he brought the glass away again, there was a white moustache of foam covering his upper lip.

The foam was still there when I came back from the Gents' a few minutes later. If anything, it had grown, into something that would not have looked out of place in the Cheltenham Conservative Club.

Mick stared at him critically, searching for the words needed to express his disapproval.

' 'ere, cunt,' he said at last. 'You've got foam all over your gob. Makes you look like a berk.'

Dave clutched his stomach with both hands, squeezed and let go with another painful belch.

'Get stuffed,' he said, when he had finished.

'I was only telling you. If you want to go around looking like a berk, go ahead. I don't give a monkey's.'

Ignoring him, Dave massaged his stomach, trying to release more of the trapped gas. Mick turned away to begin sorting moodily through a bag of crisps. His search was long and arduous, but in the end successful. Giving an audible grunt of satisfaction, he extracted the perfect potato crisp and held it up against the light for one last demanding scrutiny. It passed. He placed it in his mouth and began to chew, slowly and deliberately.

Eating the crisp produced a visible raising of his spirits. Wearing a small smile of anticipation, he set off on another search through the plastic bag. As a sort of Buddhist, I knew that his search had to end in failure and disappointment. The second crisp wasn't going to taste anywhere near as good as the first. Such is the transitory nature of sensual pleasure.

'Too much salt,' Mick complained a moment or so later.

Dave accomplished one of his lower-key belches and then turned to look at him with contempt.

'That's what makes you thirsty, innit?' he said, the foam moustache lending his words a certain authority. 'When you're thirsty, you drink more beer. Pubs sell beer. You buy it from them. The more beer you buy, the more profit the brewers make. That's why they sell crisps with salt on them. So berks like you eat them and get a thirst on. So you order up another beer and give the brewer the money to send his kids to private school. That's the way capitalism works.'

'Well, I'm hungry,' Mick complained in a whine. 'You've got to eat, haven't you? That's one of the laws of nature. You have to eat to live. Even animals have to eat to live.'

'They don't eat crisps, though, do they?' Dave pointed out.

'Dogs do. I'm always seeing dogs in pubs eating crisps. So up yours, cunt.'

Despairing of his companion, Dave turned to look around

the room. When he reached me, his gaze rested momentarily on my face. A faint flicker of recognition registered before he looked away. A small bell had gone off somewhere in his brain. Not an alarm. Just a small, vaguely puzzling tinkle. That was enough for now.

The electric clock behind the bar showed a few minutes to nine. I hoped the lads hadn't got a big evening planned. I also hoped they weren't intending to mix French blues with their beer. According to my informant, Mick and Dave were apt to turn nasty when they mixed uppers with their booze. The combination made them aggressive and confident. I didn't feel up to handling them, if they were going to be aggressive and confident.

Mick suddenly scrunched the crisp bag in one hand, tightening his grip until the knuckles whitened. When he was certain that the bag was quite dead, he let it fall to the floor before delivering a gratuitous *coup de grâce* with the toe of his Doc Martin's. The bag skittered across the worn carpeting to end up alongside the fruit machine that had so far taken eighty pee from me. Mick turned back to the bar and began a close study of a beer mat that had caught his eye.

Dave yawned. It was a long slow process that involved much stretching and a display of NHS fillings. When the yawn was finally over, he lowered one of his podgy hands to scratch his arse for a while. After that, he tried scratching his arse and yawning at the same time. But he lacked the co-ordination.

We all spent a few pleasant moments watching an agreeably overweight blonde bend over the juke box to stab a red-painted fingernail at the selection buttons. Dave expressed his appreciation of her small jiggling movements by pursing his lips and producing a noise like bathwater being sucked down a plughole. More inhibited than Dave, I watched her with nothing more than a few quiet moans.

The blonde stood up, did a little more jiggling in time to the music, then went back to her large black boyfriend. Mick scrunched the beer mat in his hand, dropped it back on the counter, then went out to the Gents'. Dave added more foam to his moustache. Unable to think of anything else to do, I rolled ten pee into the Spastics' box on the counter.

3

A man came in, carrying a small, dusty-looking dog in his arms. He put the dog on a stool and tried to engage the barmaid in a conversation about cricket. When she walked off, he tried me, with as little success. As a last resort, he turned to Dave. To our common surprise, he struck lucky. Dave was a fanatic.

Mick came back from the Gents' with one hand still doing up his flies. Dave carried on talking to the man about cricket. I put more money in the Spastics' box. If things went on like this for very much longer, I was going to make a loss on this job.

Mick bought another packet of crisps and began feeding them to the dog on the stool. He seemed to have brightened up a lot since his visit to the Gents'. His eyes had the carefree sparkle that comes from a line of coke or a couple of French blues. He looked aggressive and confident.

When the dog had finished the crisps, Mick leaned over and broke into the conversation that its owner was having with Dave.

'You ready, cunt?' he asked.

Dave opened his mouth, punched himself in the stomach and let go with another belch. The fist he punched himself with had 'right' tattooed across the back. The one wrapped around his beer glass was labelled 'left'. Mick also had tattooed letters across the backs of his hands – 'knife' on the right and 'fork' on the left.

Dave drained his glass, placed it on the counter and then patted the man's dog. The dog quivered. Dave nodded at the man and then walked over to join Mick at the door. It looked as if we were off.

Two

Mick and Dave had parked their motor bike and sidecar a little
way up the street. My battered old Citroen estate was outside
the pub. I unlocked the door and slid into a comfort belied by
the car's shabby exterior. I had bought it cheap from a man
whose concern with appearances was not matched by his
London driving skills. Mine had been his third car in as many
years since his moving here from Shropshire. He was thinking
of moving back.

Keeping an eye on Mick as he straddled the bike, I searched
around on the radio until I found some classical guitar music.
Bach. Mick seemed to be having a little trouble.

With sinking heart I watched Dave climb out of the side-car,
holding an object that glittered in the orange streetlights. A
spanner. We seemed to be shaping up for a long night.

Bach gave way to Fauré. Mick and Dave had most of the
bike's parts spread across the pavement by now. Watching
them work, I listened to a talk on Brazilian Symbolists given by
a man who sounded like he was strung out on Valium. Dave
walked over to a nearby building site to borrow a few bricks for
use as a jack, while Mick removed the back wheel. According to
the floodlit clock on the church tower opposite, it took Mick
exactly twenty-three minutes to get the wheel off.

Emotionally drained by the lecture on Brazilian Symbolists,
I punched the buttons until I found some mellow jazz piano.
Bill Evans. I had several of his records back home. Wherever
that was. I seemed to have been following Mick and Dave
around for the best part of my life.

Following a long, increasingly heated exchange of gestures
that suggested some discussion, Mick put the wheel back on.
Almost instantly he took it off again. Going against my better
judgement, I opened the glove compartment, took out a ready-
rolled joint and lit it.

The pub turned out. Tuesday night. Not many customers. A couple of tipsy old biddies clutching each other for support as they faded away up the street. An ageing hippy with a grey ponytail and a launderette bag of washing. The cricket fan stopped to have a word with Dave. He was probably trying to get him to name the entire Yorkshire team for their match against Surrey at the Oval in 1954, or something like that. Dave ignored him. The man allowed his dog to lead him away. I began to feel a small pleasant buzz from the joint.

The pub door opened and the barmaid stepped out and tilted her head, checking the sky for rain. As she set off up the street the bolts slid noisily into place behind her. Her high heels made a lonely clacking sound on the pavement. Both Dave and I had tried our luck with her, but neither of us had been successful.

Returning my attention to the lads, I found them straightening up from having replaced the wheel. Better still, they were beginning to reassemble the scattered parts of the machine. In what seemed only hours, they had it together again. Dave climbed back into the side-car, and Mick once more straddled himself over the bike. On the eighteenth attempt by my count the engine caught, roared into life and settled into a healthy throb.

Mick thought otherwise. Killing the engine, he climbed off and began tinkering around with the spanner again.

Sighing a long, despairing sigh, I turned on my ignition. When I had the car running, I turned the heating to full. It was getting cold.

There were dead leaves trapped in my windscreen wipers. It was late autumn, the dying season. Winter was only weeks away. A bad time for Leo subjects. Even for those of them who didn't place too much credence in astrology. My resistance to depression was always low this time of the year. There were ways when I could do little more than lie on my living-room carpet, staring up at the ceiling wishing I had the strength to get as far as the kitchen to make a cup of tea. As a sort of Buddhist, I knew that winter was the necessary yin to the yang of summer – just part of the eternal cycle of life, death and rebirth. But still, it always got to me.

It didn't help that even my local shops had joined in the

grand Christmas wind-up. The Indian grocer across the street from my flat had been on at me to join his 'Festive Hamper Club'. If I gave him two or three quid a week from now until December 24th he would, on that day, present me with a basketful of crystallized fruits, figs, dates, liqueur chocolates and all kinds of other things that I never eat. I told him I was hoping to go away.

I rolled down the car window to clear my head a little. The night air smelled of damp and decay. Smoking the joint had been a mistake, I decided. My mood was entering a downward spiral. I tried to think of something pleasant and failed to come up with anything.

Mick saddled up yet again and began jumping up and down on the starter. When the engine finally caught, he revved it long enough and loud enough to have someone open a window and lean out to complain. Dave told the man to get stuffed. With a sudden lurch, the bike and side-car pulled away from the kerb. I let in the clutch and began to follow.

My informant had been unable to supply an address for Mick and Dave. The best he had been able to do was give me the name of the caff where they took most of their meals. To my surprise I had found them there straight off. They had been enjoying a deep-fried brunch charred to a nicety in lavish amounts of cooking fat. I carried a cup of tea over to a nearby table and sat down. The tea tasted of disinfectant. The cup was chipped and the saucer had been used as an ashtray. When my egg and chips arrived, they tasted and looked like something that had been scraped off the underside of a long-distance lorry.

The meal over, Mick and Dave had moved on to try their luck at a nearby betting shop. The place was packed with fellow punters, and the air was thick with cigarette smoke and beery farts. A small, dried-up old man standing next to me was suddenly seized with a violent bout of coughing that had him spraying yellow phlegm over my raincoat. When he was through coughing, he borrowed my pen to make out his selection on a betting slip. He didn't apologize for infecting my raincoat with whatever disease he had. Nor did he offer to give me my pen back until I tapped him on the shoulder. If he had been forty years younger, I would have thumped him. But then, if he had been forty years younger, he would probably have beaten the shit out of me. He was a vicious-looking old sod.

Mick and Dave had spent the next couple of hours backing their fancies with amounts that never exceeded fifty pee. For a couple of guys sitting around on three thousand quidsworth of Paki Black, they were small spenders. Seventy pee ahead, they decided it was time to quit. I felt a need to lie down and recover from all the excitement. But it was back to the caff for another cup of tea.

As we sipped at what my Gran always called the cup that cheers but never inebriates, Dave read aloud from an evening newspaper someone had left behind. He didn't read well. His style was somewhat slow and hesitant. But the items he choose to read out were punctuated with much pithy comment on the anomalies and injustices of the British social system. To be honest, I often found myself agreeing with him.

Afternoon tea over, it was off to see a rerun of 'The Return of the Jedi.' Not being a sci-fi buff, I drew the line at actually going in with them. Instead I checked the screening time and picked them up as they came out afterwards. From what I heard of their conversation, they had enjoyed it. If anything, they both thought 'Return of the Jedi' was even better than 'The Empire Strikes Back'. Mick had wanted to see it round again. But Dave's hunger had won out. It was back to the caff.

I ordered baked beans on toast and got them on fried bread. My tea came in the same unwashed cup and saucer. And the tea itself was probably the same stuff I had left almost untouched earlier, just reheated. Dave seemed well pleased with his double egg, spaghetti, sausage and chips. But he wisely obliterated any possible flavour by emptying most of the contents of a sauce bottle over his plate. Mick settled for a more spartan repast – two slices of toast. He had probably ordered fried bread.

Neither of them noticed that I had been following them around for the best part of the day. I was wondering whether to feel insulted or not when Dave had got up to lead the way to the pub.

Now, as I fiddled with the car radio, trying to clear a burst of static, ahead of me Mick and Dave turned off into a sidestreet. I followed and watched them park outside a house covered in builders' scaffolding. There were lights on in the basement and on the first floor. The rest of the house was in darkness. I parked and waited for a light to go on in one of the upper windows. When it did, I got out of my car and walked over to the house.

There was a row of buzzers alongside the front door, without any names. Using a trick from one of my many self-improvement books, I went into alpha and let my instincts take over. When I felt that they'd had enough time to make up their minds, I jabbed a button at random.

To my astonishment Mick answered the door. But the explanation was provided by the milk bottle he held in his hand, preparatory to putting it out on the doorstep.

'Yeah?' he questioned, putting the empty bottle alongside a row of others.

My outfit had been selected to suggest vague connections with officialdom and authority. I wore a fawn raincoat, the official school tie of St Winifred's School for Young Ladies (thirty pee from a junk shop in Clapham), and a dark blue suit from C & A. My white shoes probably clashed with the image I was hoping to project, but they are a weakness with me. I wear white shoes just about all the time. It is possible that I was a Spanish waiter in a previous incarnation.

'Hello, Mick,' I greeted him, with what I hoped was worrying familiarity.

He frowned and stared at me closely in the light thrown by the overhead fitting.

'Am I supposed to know you or something?' he asked. Something slowly edged its way into his consciousness. ' 'ere, you've been following us about. You were in the pub.' He frowned again. 'And you was in the caff.'

'And I was in the betting shop when you took the bookies for a cool seventy pee. You had me biting my nails down to my elbows.'

'What's your game, then?' he asked, trying to sound aggressive and confident. But the business with the motor cycle had taken it out of him.

'Why don't we talk about it inside?' I suggested.

'Talk about what?'

I gave a long theatrical sigh and shook my head. When I had finished doing that, I gave him a nasty smile.

'We're going to talk about that three pounds of Paki Black you and your mate knocked off from Anita's place.'

Mick looked like a man overtaken by a sudden and terminal illness.

'You a copper?' he asked fearfully.

'Detective Sergeant Skindle, West End Central,' I replied, employing the name and rank of a bent ex-member of the force I'd once had dealings with.

'I don't know what you're talking about,' Mick tried, without a lot of hope.

'You mean you've never heard of West End Central?'

'No. I mean the Paki Black. I don't know anything about that. Honest.'

A woman holding a hot-water bottle in her hand came out and stood in the hallway looking at us for a while. I showed her my nasty smile and she went back inside.

'This doesn't have to be strictly official,' I told Mick. 'Not unless you want it to be. I'm sure we can find a way of fixing it to everybody's satisfaction. Now, are you going to invite me in?' I asked, as he stood hesitating. 'Or shall I be sending for uniformed assistance and a couple of hash puppies to sniff the stuff out?'

Mick reluctantly arrived at his decision.

'Alright,' he agreed. 'But I don't know what you're talking about.'

'Bollocks. Don't piss me about, son,' I warned, in what I thought was a good impersonation of Skindle's style. 'I've got acid indigestion from eating in that caff of yours. Don't make my mood any worse.'

Still making little whimpering protestations of innocence, Mick led me up an uncarpeted flight of stairs. On the first-floor landing we encountered a broken, sagging couch bearing a figure huddled in a sleeping bag. There was a strong smell of old socks. Mick turned and led the way up another flight of stairs. At the top of them was an open door.

'Who was it?' Dave called out from somewhere inside the flat.

10

'Skindle of the Yard,' I called back in ringing tones, realising I was still stoned from the joint I had smoked earlier.

We went in to find Dave sitting at a wooden kitchen table in front of an uncurtained window. There was an open tin of sardines in front of him and a loaf of 'Mother's Pride'. A light snack. It had been a good two hours since he had last eaten.

'Pig,' he stated, looking up at me. 'He's been following us about. I remember him now. He was sitting behind us when we saw *Return of the Jedi.*'

'Well, why didn't you say something?' Mick snapped.

'I wasn't sure, was I?' I didn't think the pigs wore white shoes.'

'Cunt. You've dropped us right in it.'

'What do you mean, I've dropped us in it? We haven't done nothing. We're innocent citizens. He's invading our bloody privacy. We could have him for that.'

He stared at me with a worrying amount of confidence. He had taken his leather jacket off to reveal a 'Motorhead' tee-shirt stretched tight over his fat-boy tits. Pushing a slice of bread aside, he lit a cigarette. Behind him late-night traffic raced home along a flyover. He broke the matchstick in his fingers and looked at me again.

'Where is it?' I asked him.

'Where's what?' He carried on smoking, seemingly unworried.

I leaned over the table.

'Where is it?' I repeated in a hard voice.

'Fuck off.'

I smacked the cigarette out of his mouth with an open hand. As he began to react, I brought the back of my hand against his cheek, knocking him from his chair.

'Don't piss me about, son,' I warned in my Skindle voice. 'I've had a hard day. I could turn nasty. You wouldn't like me when I'm nasty.'

My action had the right shock effect, making it almost worth the burns I had sustained on my fingers. Dave's confidence had slipped back into bed, pulling the sheet over its head. Dave looked up at me, white-faced from a combination of fear and anger.

'That's fucking police brutality,' he claimed. 'I could have you for that. I could have the Civil Liberties lot onto you.'

'You'd be better off working it up into a bit of performance art, or street theatre. You might even get an Arts Council grant.'

'We've had one Arts Council grant already this year,' Mick told me seriously, scratching his chin with the hand labelled 'fork'. 'I don't think you can get two in the same year.'

'Never mind that,' I snapped, with the vehemence of one who had had several Arts Council grant applications turned down. Where's the Paki Black?'

'What happens if we give it to you?' Dave asked, from where he still sat on the floor. 'Just supposing we had it, that is.'

'Nothing. Like I said – this isn't strictly official. At least, it doesn't have to be.'

Dave carried on looking at me warily. His lip was beginning to puff a little, but it probably didn't hurt as much as my fingers. I was about to ask him for some butter to put on them when he spoke.

'Alright,' he sighed. 'Fuck it. Give it to him.'

Mick went over to one of a pair of single beds, both covered in pink nylon. He rolled the cover back, crawled underneath, then came out again holding a plastic shopping bag. He brought the bag over and gave it to me.

'Is it all here?' I asked, sternly.

'We've had a few smokes out of it,' he admitted. 'But that's all. We hadn't worked out how we were going to sell it.'

I checked the bag. It didn't seem as if there was much missing.

'We only did it because we were pissed,' Mick said, already rehearsing his defence plea. 'We went round to Anita's to score off her. After we'd been in the pub. She wasn't in. Her door looked easy so we thought we'd go in and help ourselves to a quarter and settle up with her later. We didn't mean to take all of it. It just sort of happened.'

'He doesn't want to know all that bollocks,' Dave sneered, climbing to his feet. 'You stupid berk. You've gone and dropped Anita in it now.

'He doesn't know who Anita is.'

'He soon will with your bloody help.'

'I didn't say where she lives, cunt. There's a lot of Anitas about.'

'There's a lot of pillocks around, too. And you're one of them.'

Dave's nose was running. For a moment I thought it was blood. But it was only snot. He dabbed at it with the sleeve of his tee-shirt. Mick stood at his side, watching me worriedly. His Mohican was going thin in places, and most of his face was covered in acne. They were such a pathetic pair of berks that I found myself beginning to feel sorry for them.

'You got any skins?' I asked.

Dave looked at me suspiciously.

'It's not illegal to have fag papers on the premises,' he protested. 'You can't touch us for that.'

'I want to roll a joint,' I said. 'Just to make sure this stuff is genuine. I wouldn't like to think you were passing me off with rabbit shit, or something like that.'

Mick dug into his pocket with the hand labelled 'knife' and came up with a packet of Rizlas. Helping myself to one of Dave's cigarettes, I sprinkled tobacco into a couple of gummed papers and warmed an edge of hash with his plastic lighter. When the hash had softened, I crumbled a generous amount into the tobacco and then sealed the papers into a near perfect tube.

Mick and Dave watched spellbound.

'They run classes at Hendon Police College,' I told them. 'You don't get a pass until you can do it blindfold.'

I lit the joint, took a couple of puffs, then offered it to Dave.

'Piss off,' he said, his tiny blue eyes sharp with distrust. 'You're planting evidence. As soon as I take a drag, the door's going to be broken in by a herd of charging pigs.'

'Take it. No one's going to bust you. Pig's honour.'

Dave expressed his opinion of a policeman's oath by giving a cynical snort, but in the end he reached out for the joint warily. He puffed on it uneasily for a moment or two, as if waiting for it to explode like some joke shop novelty. When nothing happened, he passed it over to Mick.

'What's your game, then?' he asked, as I began rolling another joint. 'I've heard a lot of things. But I've never heard about the filth sitting around rolling joints for you.'

'It's a public relations exercise. The force has been getting a lot of bad publicity recently, one way or another. We called in Saatchi and Saatchi to improve our image. This was one of their ideas.'

'Aren't you going to take us in, then?' Mick asked, relaxing a little.

'Course he bloody isn't,' Dave sneered. 'That stuff he's got there will be back on the streets again tomorrow. He's bent. Just like all the other fuckers in the capitalist system. Pigs are just licensed villains.'

'Now then,' I cautioned. 'Show a little respect for the representatives of law and order.'

But Dave was away.

'Capitalism,' he complained bitterly. 'All it does is breed corruption and inequality. Instead of working for the common good, it just brings out the worst in people. Every fucker's out to exploit his fellow man. They're all at it. The pigs, politicians, the church –'

'The Arts Council,' I prompted as he hesitated.

'No. They're alright,' he conceded. 'You've got to have art.'

I lit the joint and stood up. On impulse I reached into the bag and broke off a lump of hash. I put it on the table.

'What's that for?' Dave asked, suspiciously.

'An early Christmas present. Something to restore your faith in human nature. Please don't thank me. I embarrass easily.'

I left them standing there, staring at the small lump of hash, neither of them daring to pick it up. I only hoped they didn't end up flushing it down the john. As a sort of Buddhist, I didn't approve of waste.

Three

There was a sharp ground frost when I awoke around eight-thirty next morning. My pot plants looked distinctly unhappy. I carried them over to the electric fire, but their mottled leaves remained listless. There was no fooling them. They knew winter was on the way. In a further effort at encouragement, I thought pleasant thoughts about them as I showered and shaved. When I came out of the bathroom, they looked a touch better.

It was late for me to be rising. Normally I am awake by six-thirty or seven. Late though it was, I set about my normal routine of Tai Chi and breathing exercises, followed by thirty to forty minutes of meditation. There was once a time when I used to rise at five, to chant mantras. But my very straight next-door neighbours asked, in the nicest possible way, if I would refrain from using my electric power drill quite so early in the morning.

When I had finished my meditation, I carried the good feelings into my day, breakfasting slowly on muesli, whole-wheat toast and sesame spread. With my Red Zinger tea I swallowed a couple of grams of ginseng. My system humming with good vibes and nourishment, I rang Anita to say I had her dope. She sounded pleased. But I sensed trouble about my fee. I could tell it irked her to think of my making £600 for less than a couple of days work. I told her I would be around in an hour or so and hung up.

I have a flat above a Greek restaurant in Camden Town. As a sort of Buddhist I am also a sort of vegetarian, but I don't object to the smell of charcoal-grilled meat that drifts upstairs during opening hours. There are times when I fall by the wayside and enjoy a meal down there myself, incurring bad karma but tasting great cooking.

When I bought the flat many years ago, there was a shoe repairer operating underneath, and if you wanted a *Guardian* you had to walk as far as Primrose Hill. At that time I had been going to set up home with a lady singer who had a bluesy voice that made me weak at the knees. But she left me before the ink was dry on the estate agent's papers, going off with an abrasive young satirist she had met while doing the Edinburgh Fringe. The abrasive young satirist ended up as compère of quiz games on children's television, and the lady singer gave up her career to become the Gruppenführer of a women's lib resistance cell. I still see her from time to time on my television screen. She's usually throwing a flour bomb or being dragged off by a couple of uniformed police. Whenever I see her, I feel pleased she isn't sharing my flat.

There was a cheering bright sun to greet me as I stepped out of my front door. The frost had cleared, and it was warm enough to fool you into thinking it was spring. At least, that was the impression given by George, one of the Greek waiters who sat on a dustbin holding his face up into the warm rays. We exchanged a few pleasantries, and I managed to keep a straight face as he told me his selections for the afternoon's racing. All the same, I borrowed a pen from him to jot down the names of horses. Just in case. George seemed not a little pleased at this. His pleasure was expressed by sending a short, fast right to my nearest bicep. My arm immediately went numb.

Flashing him a macho grin to show he hadn't hurt me, I walked over to my car. With my right arm incapable of operating, I was forced to fumble around, opening the door with my left hand. Unable to manipulate the controls with my usual authority, I pulled away from the kerb in a series of short hops. Looking into the rear-view mirror, I could see George watching me with contempt. He would probably go inside to tell the others I drove like a woman.

Four

'What happened to your arm?' Anita asked, as I handed her the bag. 'Did those boys give you any trouble?'

I started to say no and then thought better of it. Anita would prefer to think I had worked hard for my fee.

'Not a lot,' I shrugged. 'Just a couple of bruises. It's what I get paid for.'

'Well, they're certainly not going to score off me again,' Anita said angrily. 'What a nerve, breaking in here and stealing.'

'It was after the pub. They were pissed. You know how it is.'

'No, I don't. I don't drink.'

Anita began checking the contents of the bag. I moved a toy train from a settee covered in blue corduroy and sat down. Behind the settee, on a white-painted shelf, was a leather-bound frame containing a photograph of two children squinting into the sun. The girl took after her long-departed father, while the boy had the same frizzy red hair and veal-like skin of his mother. There was something unhealthy-looking about Anita. She had an air that suggested the less appealing aspects of fin-de-siècle decadence. It was easy to imagine her lurking around one of the more morbid Pre-Raphaelite painters, or haunting somebody's East Wing. I had heard that she was partial to having it off in a silk-lined coffin she kept in her bedroom. This could have just been malicious gossip, but it wouldn't have surprised me.

Anita looked up from the bag.

'It's a teensy bit short, isn't it?' she said.

'Natural spillage. It's been moving around. There's bound to be some wastage. Not a lot. No more than an ounce at most.'

Anita nodded unconvinced and returned her attention to the bag. Judging by her reputation, she would be able to estimate what was missing down to the nearest milligram. She was astute. But as a woman on her own with two children to bring up, she had to be.

Anita finally put the bag down and remembered the social niceties. Her pale fragile hand moved through the air, coming to rest at last on a china teapot covered in a design of pale blue flowers. Raising the pot, she poured tea into matching cups. The sugar I declined was proffered in a silver bowl. For someone who lived in a housing association flat, Anita had a lot of style.

'Is your fee still the same?' she enquired, handing me one of the cups.

'Yes, it is.'

'That doesn't seem entirely fair.'

'It's the figure we agreed upon. My standard fee – twenty percent.'

I took a sip of my tea. Supermarket floorsweepings.

'But it took you so little time,' Anita protested.

'It has to be that way,' I said. 'If you don't find the stuff quickly, chances are you won't find it at all. The sort of people I'm hired to go after get rid of the stuff quickly. They're always small-timers. They scare easy and want to unload it as quickly as they can. For most of them, it's their first venture into this kind of thing. Mick and Dave breaking into your place when they were pissed is typical.'

Anita was unconvinced.

'All the same. Six hundred pounds. You must be very rich.'

I laughed without humour.

'I've got an overdraft and a car I can't afford to run. This sort of job turns up on average two or three times a year. The rest of the time I'm an unsuccessful painter. Financially unsuccessful, anyway. Even more so now I've lost the teaching job I had. I was declared redundant. Just think of yourself as a patroness of the arts.'

Someone in an upstairs flat began hoovering. I thought it was an improvement on the noise coming from Anita's budgerigars. As the hoovering continued, Anita winced, got up from her chair and switched on a radio, filling the room with a sudden burst of no-holds-barred grand opera. I signalled for her to turn it down. Coming back to her chair, Anita stepped on a lump of plasticine. She sighed, sat down and began removing it from the sole of her shoe.

'I'm sorry about the state of the place,' she apologized, making me feel like a health visitor or a social worker. 'I just don't get the time.'

'It looks fine to me.'

'It's dreadful,' she insisted. 'I haven't cleaned properly in days. It's so hard to keep up with housework, and deal, and bring up two small children.'

'Listen, my place has never looked this good.' Anita rolled the plasticine into a ball and dropped it into an ashtray.

'Do you know,' she continued, 'I get so tired sometimes, I have to take a line of sulphate just to get through the washing-up.'

'It's a tough old world. Look, I have to be going.'

'Ah yes, your money.' From her tone it was clear that if the housing association flat possessed a tradesman's entrance, that was where our business would be conducted.

Anita lifted her shoe again to scrape away more plasticine from her sole. Her underwear was red. With many women I would have found the view titillating. With Anita I found myself looking the other way.

'Will a cheque be alright?' she asked, after a while.

'You did say cash. I made you repeat it after me. Twice. It was agreed we could walk round to the bank together.'

Anita gave me a smile and giggled in what she probably thought was an appealing way.

'I did say that, didn't I. But that was before.'

'Before what?'

'Before I found out that I had miscalculated how much I had in my account. I can't get the hang of these pocket calculators.'

'Sure you can't, Anita.'

'Anyway, you'll never guess.' She gave a peal of laughter that was probably mean to sound like tinkling bells or a brook swollen by the spring rains.

'I think I can guess, actually. You're overdrawn.'

Anita clapped her hands together, crying, 'Oh, well done that man.' She bared her dingy teeth at me again. 'But there's nothing to worry about.'

'You've got the money stashed away in a coffee jar.'

'Not exactly. But now I'm back in business again, I should be able to pay you in two or three days at the most.'

I was about to reply when the doorbell rang. Anita looked at me puzzled.

'Who could that be?' she asked.

'Perhaps it's the bank manager come to tell you about a bank error in your favour.'

Anita emitted a subdued shriek, followed by a low moan.

'Shit,' she said. 'It's her.'

'Who?'

'Aunt Adele,' she explained impatiently. 'She's come for lunch. I'd completely forgotten. What will I do?'

'See if you can borrow six hundred quid off her,' I said, unsympathetically.

'No. Don't go,' Anita said, pushing me back onto the couch as I began to rise. 'She'll only think we've been having it off together or something, if you rush away. She's got a truly evil mind. Quick, switch on the air-extractor in case she smells the dope.'

Confused, I turned to grapple with the workings of a small air-extractor resting on a table by the side of the couch. I could hear voices in the hallway. By the time I found the switch to work the air-extractor Aunt Adele was there, looking critically around the room. I stood up.

'Aunt Adele. This is Stan. Stan Garland. A friend of mine.'

Aunt Adele stood watching me, wearing the same, faint, mocking smile Jack Palance had worn sizing up Alan Ladd in 'Shane'. Like Jack Palance, she too was all decked out in black like a gunfighter. The fingers of her hands curled loose and easy over the top of a large, black leather handbag. When she felt she had my number, Aunt Adele gave me a demonstration of her fast draw.

'Do you have a job?' she enquired, in an accent from across the Scots border.

'Not at the moment,' I admitted. 'But, I'm expecting a sum of money. It should have been here today.'

Aunt Adele waved my explanation aside with one of her black-gloved hands.

'I asked,' she continued, narrowing the smile by a millimetre or so, 'because it seems quite the fashion to live off the State these days.'

'That could have something to do with the Government's economic policy, don't you think?' I said, keeping the tone as pleasant as I could.

The smile snapped shut.

'There's always work available for those that want it. Most of Anita's friends seem to prefer lying in bed until all hours, sponging off others.'

'Stan had a real job,' Anita offered. 'He was an art teacher. Until he was made redundant.'

'Really?' Aunt Adele nodded her head in a satirical gesture of being impressed. 'And what do you do now?'

'I paint.'

'Just paint?'

'That's right. I just paint. Like Picasso, Titian, Degas, Bonnard and all the rest of them.'

She was not impressed.

'You can hardly, I am sure, lay claim to the talent of the people you have just mentioned. It seems a very precarious way of life. Especially for a man of your age.' Her merciless eyes took a leisurely trip around my face, stopping off for an examination of various wrinkles and lines before coming to rest on my thinning hair. 'How old are you now?' she asked. 'Forty-seven or eight? Older perhaps?'

'Forty,' I snapped.

'Really?' Her crudely drawn eyebrows rose like Van Gogh crows. 'You look a lot older. You haven't got the sort of face that ages well. Not, I should imagine, that it could ever have been described as handsome.'

'Someone once said it was the sort of face you find on an old coin at the bottom of the sea. I think she was being complimentary.'

Aunt Adele smiled pityingly.

'Men are so easily flattered,' she said.

'Well, I must tear myself away,' I said. 'I'd say it was nice meeting you, but I'd be lying through my teeth.'

I walked out into the hall.

'Why do you put up with her?' I asked Anita on the doorstep. 'She's an evil old cow.'

'I'm hoping she'll leave me money in her will,' she said.

'I wouldn't bet on it. She'll probably leave it to a home for retired police dogs.'

'Look,' Anita said. 'Come round this evening and I might be able to give you some money on account.' She had a sudden thought. 'Not this evening. I've got a Tupperware party.'

'A Tupperware party?' I echoed incredulously.

'Yes. Give me a ring tomorrow.'

I took my foot away, and the door closed in my face. Maybe Anita had set the whole thing up with her aunt, I thought, walking away. Even now they could be splitting the stash down the middle, congratulating themselves on how well they had handled me.

I'd be around bright and early tomorrow, I promised myself. Bright and early, with the iron bar in my raincoat pocket. Just in case Aunt Adele was still around.

Five

I was still thinking about Aunt Adele when I decided to go to my kung fu club that evening. Not that it was a place to work out aggression. On the contrary, my instructor Master Hu Feng frowned upon aggression and anger. He found both a form of weakness. 'A man who loses his temper loses the fight' was one of his many maxims. But then Master Hu Feng hadn't met Aunt Adele.

It was a quiet night at the club. Only a dozen or so were there. Self-improvement seemed to be somewhat less popular than getting pissed in front of the telly. I worked out with a short, chunky nurse who managed to catch me with a couple of kicks. The second hurt like buggery, but I managed to show nothing more than an inscrutable smile as I shoved a Leopard Fist at her left kidney. The nurse evaded me with ease. And as I wobbled past her off-balance, she scooped my legs from under me.

'You're out of practice,' she said, adding to my humiliation by helping me up from the floor. 'I usually beat you. But not as easily as that.'

'You're not very far along the path if you still think in terms of winning and losing,' I countered.

But she had gone; off to the other side of the room, to work out with a lanky Australian called Fred.

I sat down on one of the chairs lining the walls. The hall the club was held in was owned by the Quakers. The rent was cheap and the heating minimal. I pushed my back against a radiator. It took a while, but eventually I felt a tepid warmth coming through my tee-shirt. I sighed and closed my eyes.

'What's this, Stan? You gone and died on me?' The voice was the sort you usually hear on market stalls selling dodgy goods, and the accent was pure London.

'Have a heart, Master Feng. I'm knackered,' I protested.

I opened my eyes. The man looking down at me was short and stocky with powerful forearms thrusting out of the short sleeves of his black training jacket. He was bald except for a fringe of white hair starting just above his ears, and his features had an Oriental cast. Rumour had it that he was seventy years old. But that was hard to believe when you saw him in class. The speed of his movements, as he executed a kick or a strike, was phenomenal.

'You won't learn anything sitting there, Stan. Rest is for the sick and the old.'

'How about the tired.'

'You only think you're tired. It's just a trick of the mind. Come on, up on your feet.'

I rose to my feet. Master Hu Feng bowed, then came at me with a series of lightning strikes and kicks – none of which I managed to stop or evade. Fortunately he pulled the power back, connecting on the various parts of my body with nothing more than a sharp tap.

Some evening this was turning out to be. First I had had the shit beaten out of me by a short, overweight nurse. Now I was being clobbered at will by a septuagenarian.

The septuagenarian stopped hitting me, stepped a pace backwards and bowed.

I bowed back. Just to show there were no hard feelings.

'You're getting out of nick,' he said, as we stood watching the nurse apply a painful wristlock on Australian Fred.

'I don't know why. I've been working out everyday. Even if I haven't been getting to the club as often as I want to.'

Australian Fred tapped up, but the nurse appeared not to notice. And it wasn't until he shouted out, 'You're breaking my bloody wrist, you stupid tart,' that she released her hold.

'What about your diet?' Master Feng asked. 'You been eating any junk?'

I hesitated. I have never subscribed to the more far-out of the claims that those in the club are apt to bandy between kicks, concerning Master Feng's psychic abilities. But he did seem to have a way of knowing things sometimes. So I admitted to a couple of hamburgers and a sausage roll.

'Well, I suppose a bit of yang won't do you any harm now

and then,' he said. 'As long as you balance it with some yin.'

'I have given up drinking,' I said, pleased.

Australian Fred had gone to sit down, holding his wrist and massaging it gently. He seemed to be in considerable pain. The nurse had moved onto Simon, a gangly, greying teacher who was trying to overcome a lifelong fear of contact sports. The nurse struck through his feeble ward-off and hit him with a Sword Hand, extended fingers jabbing into his ribcage. I was glad she had only used me for a warm-up.

'Given up drinking have you? For how long?'

'A month,' I said. 'But even before that I was only drinking white wine.'

'Very yin, wine,' Master Hu Feng said, uncompromisingly. 'Too much of it can do you a right nasty. I know from experience.'

'You? A drinker?' I asked incredulously.

'Not me. My father. Well, my adopted father. He wasn't Chinese. He was a Londoner. A good man, but he couldn't control his need for alcohol. It did for him in the end. I've never touched a drop.'

His story might have been all the more effective, had I not on several occasions seen Master Feng consume a variety of alcoholic drinks. My guru not only had feet of clay, he also possessed an impaired memory. It was hard to separate truth from fantasy at times. Especially when he went on about his astral travels. I wasn't as convinced of his being able to do this as other members of the club were. Especially some of the female members.

The greying teacher hopped over to a chair, holding his knee, face contorted with pain. The nurse followed him to employ her professional skills in an examination of the damage she had done.

'I'll have to have a word with Sandra,' Master Feng said. 'She's getting a bit over-enthusiastic.'

'Too yang altogether,' I agreed.

Later, while I was having a drink with some of the club members in the pub opposite, one of the girls told me that Master Feng kept astral-tripping into her bedroom at night. I'd heard this story so often from various female members that I began to wonder if there might be some truth in it. Maybe I could get him show me how to astral-trip myself. It would be an invaluable aid in my sometime profession of alternative private eye.

Six

It was fine again next morning, with a fat orange sun hanging in a near-cloudless blue sky. I rang Anita when I had finished working out (allowing another twenty minutes for the new deep breathing programme I had inaugurated in view of my poor performance at the club the previous evening.) Anita was not only in, but promised to have money for me by midday.

George, the Greek waiter, was sitting on the dustbin, smoking a cigarette again. He called me over for my opinion of the horses he had marked in the racing pages of the *Sun*. I told him 'My Man Stan' in the three twenty might be worth a flutter, and he punched me in the arm, making me drop my car keys. As I pulled away from the kerb, working the controls once again with my left hand, George called out for Alexis to come and watch.

Ever punctual by nature, I was at Anita's by eleven forty-five. When there was no reply to my ringing, I assumed she was at the bank. I sat on the front wall outside the house enjoying the sun. I watched a C11 bus go by. It was a rare sight around these parts. When I had watched two more pass, I realised Anita was not going to keep our appointment.

Anita had done a bunk, and 'My Man Stan' failed to feature in the first three horses past the post.

I seemed to be moving into a heavy yin period.

Seven

I had known No. 83 Caulfield Road when it was a workmen's caff serving what had to be the finest bubble-and-squeak in North London. Many of my breakfasts had been taken there. The owner, an amiable Scot who had been a professional boxer in his youth, always sent a drink over when he spotted me across the bar of our joint local.

I had been much taken by his never changing greeting – 'How's yuir luck?' – always delivered with total sincerity and interest. So taken was I with the bonhomie and warmth of his greeting, I even adopted it myself for a while. But I lacked both the accent and the genuine interest in each and every one of my fellow men. That was before I became a sort of Buddhist, of course. Now I try harder. As Lao Tsu says, the journey of a thousand miles begins with the first step.

Harry, the Scot, sold his caff when the area began to show the first signs of gentrification. He carted his wife off to live in a mobile home in the West Country. I missed his greeting. And I missed his bubble-and-squeak.

He sent me a postcard once. Knowing me to be of an artistic bent, he had chosen the postcard with great care. It depicted three airbrush work kittens, each wearing a smock, a beret and a Vandyke beard, painting away at portraits of mice. I couldn't decipher the writing on the other side, but I was touched by the thought.

The bright young things who bought Harry out turned the place into a bistro: 'Chez Julian'. I ate there once and paid four times the price for a Shepherd's Pie that Harry wouldn't have given to his dog.

'Chez Julian' gave way to 'Justin Time', a camp horologist. And when the sand ran swiftly into the bottom of his hourglass, he sold out to 'La Femme de Boulanger'.

'La Femme de Boulanger' was owned and run by a large,

butch-looking Canadian woman, who was just a little ahead of the trend. There weren't enough of us in the area to make profitable her policy of only selling fancy breads, croissants and expensive pastries. Ours was sliced white bread country back in those days, and 'Mother's Pride' reigned supreme. The butch-looking Canadian woman was ahead of the trend in another aspect also – the area wasn't ready for its first uncloseted dyke.

Next we had 'Grated Expectations'. It belonged to an extremist breakaway group from the Vegan Society, and its uncompromising, strictly limited menu had the place closed in weeks. They sold out to 'Gallery 83'.

'Gallery 83' was run by a couple of ex-media folk who didn't know a lot about art, but knew everything there was to know about using contacts. They exploited and presumed even on the slightest acquaintance. They had no shame.

They didn't mind that the people who turned up for the private views – minor TV faces and assorted trendies – knew even less about art than they themselves did. Just so long as the punters had money they could be separated from. As one of their regular exhibitors who sold from time to time, I wasn't entirely against their attitude. Live and let live. Each to their own karma.

I had three paintings in that night's private viewing. I needed to sell one of them at least, just to keep going, now that Anita had pissed off without paying me. I hoped that Judd and Carrie would be on good form. Even more, I hoped that they weren't going to get smashed, as they sometimes did, and have one of their screaming brawls.

I found the bar and poured myself an orange squash, wishing my hosts had the courtesy to serve Perrier water for nouveau teetotallers like myself. I was swilling the liquid around in my glass, pondering on the nature of the chemicals that could produce such an unnatural shade of orange, when a voice spoke into my ear.

'Hey, Babes,' it said. 'You're not going to put that stuff inside your system voluntarily are you?'

I turned to see myself reflected in a pair of dark mirror glasses. My huge head tapered away to a tiny pair of feet, making me look like a player in some corny avant-garde movie.

'Hello, Captain,' I greeted the spectre behind the glasses. 'What brings a man of your jaded taste and sensibilities to a place like this?'

'Art. I'm getting into Art. I feel this sudden need for culture in my life. I thought I'd come and dig your stuff.'

Captain Midnight reached around me, extended a long, thin hand and lowered it, like a penny arcade grabber, onto a miniature sausage roll. He raised the roll to mouth level, swallowed it and chewed with little visible pleasure.

'The catering would rate a mechanic's glove in the Egon Ronay guide. That was terrible,' he said, brushing crumbs from his mouth.

Captain Midnight is a mixture of more races than anyone has ever been able to establish. He claims to have Irish, French, Barbadian, Turkish and Greek blood pumping around his drugged system. Just about all nationalities on earth seem to have made it with one another sometime or other along his family line – regardless of race, creed or politics. The evidence is there in the long, skeletal frame covered in pale, coffee-coloured skin, topped with hair that looks like a heap of grated carrot resting on his head. His eyes, which I saw once when Captain Midnight needed to wipe a smear from his dark glasses, are a piercing green.

Captain Midnight feels that his unique ancestry gives him a deep understanding of human nature. He is a deeply cynical fellow who lives off human folly. No scrap of gossip is too trivial for his ears. No rumour is without interest. He knows everything that is going on. And where. And with whom. The information he gathers is for sale to the highest bidder. He is loyal to no one. Captain Midnight is an untrustworthy person.

He seems to have no fixed place of abode, no pillow on which to rest his carrot-coloured head. If you want to contact him, you have to leave a message on his telephone answering service. He will get back to you, almost invariably, within two hours of your call. The Ford Fairlane, in which he seems to live, will glide to a halt outside the restaurant at which you are eating for the first time. A discreet honk on the three-toned horn will rouse you from a strange bed to find the Ford Fairlane waiting in the street below.

Captain Midnight will never tell you how he managed to find you. If you ask, he just chuckles irritatingly and changes the subject, or gets you to roll a joint for him while he's driving.

Away from the car, Captain Midnight always seems ill at ease. His fingers drum constantly on the nearest surface, and his gaze keeps shifting around. He rarely stays long. His visits are as fleeting as the rest periods of a butterfly.

He took a sip of wine and spat it back into the glass.

'These pips are the pits,' he complained. 'The grape is going ape. And the wine is far from fine –'

'Knock it off, Captain,' I interrupted. 'I can't stand that rap shit. I've had a hard day. I'm feeling irritable.'

Captain Midnight put the wine back on the cloth-covered table and picked up a small triangular sandwich.

'The catering is definitely inferior,' he pronounced after chewing for a moment or two. 'This shit is not going to put the art lovers in the frame of mind for scribbling in their cheque books. I speak as a friend. Shoot your caterer.'

Judd Gleason lumbered over to pick up a bottle of wine from the table. He was large and fleshy, with a mop of shaggy grey hair and a nose like W.C. Fields. His face was red and sweating and he knocked over several glasses reaching for the wine bottle.

'I wouldn't touch that piss, Babes,' Captain Midnight advised, as Judd made a swaying examination of the label. 'It'll melt the dirt in your toenails.

'Finest Spanish plonk,' Judd said, with the careful enunciation of a drunk who wasn't far off his bedtime. 'I never drink anything else. It gets you pissed. What else do you want from a drink? If you can't get pissed out of your skull every now and then, what's the point of living?'

He stood glaring at us belligerently for a moment or two, then lumbered off. Probably to pick a fight with his wife Carrie.

I turned to Captain Midnight.

'Thanks a lot,' I said bitterly. 'That was one of the owners of this place.'

'Yeah, I know,' Captain Midnight said calmly. 'He's getting

smashed because this place is losing money like there's no tomorrow. They are in big trouble.'

'I thought they were doing alright,' I protested.

'Nah. Not recently. You've joined their list of promising youngish painters at the wrong time. They're just one step away from having their nuts chewed off by the official receiver.'

He took out a joint and lit it. I started to caution him then realised that the people there wouldn't care even if they happened to notice.

'Shit. You've done a great job on cheering me up,' I said. 'Do you have anything to make me feel worse?'

Captain Midnight inhaled deeply, then handed the joint over to me.

'You're going to have trouble getting your bread from that Anita chick,' he said, as he let the smoke out of his lungs.

'That's what I thought. Where is she?'

'She's packed up and gone off to Dumfries with her aunt. She won't be around for a while. The filth have been active around her area. She's being cautious. Pretty smart chick.'

'Very smart. She took the dope with her, I suppose.'

'Yep. She'll have no trouble unloading it up in Porridgeville. She's sharp and cool. And she's played you for a fool.'

'If you start another rap, I'm going for a crap.'

'Sorry, Babes.'

He snapped his fingers, indicating I should return the joint. I passed it to him.

Across the other side of the room I could see Judd making a fool of himself to a couple of bit-part actors and their wives. I looked around for Carrie and saw her leaning heavily for support on a man who was looking embarrassed. I had a feeling I wasn't going to sell any paintings.

'That is definite, is it?' I asked. 'About Anita.'

'You may consider that information one hundred percent correct. I drove them all to the station myself, her, her aunt and the kids.'

'You drove them?' I said, surprised. 'How did that come about?'

'Like that other fellow, Captain Midnight moves in mysterious ways. For professional reasons, he finds himself unable to answer your question.'

'What about the aunt? Was she in on it?'

'Nah. She's just an aunt. You tripping out on this grass already?'

'At the risk of sounding offensive, I would suggest that Captain Midnight is not being entirely honest in his dealing with me.'

He smiled and handed back the joint.

'Captain Midnight is not entirely honest in his dealings with anyone,' he said. 'That is why you can trust him.'

'That has the ring of a Zen koan. I think it's going to take me a couple of hundred years to work it out.'

While I stood smoking, Captain Midnight moved over to examine a painting hanging on one of the walls. Some six feet by four and executed in garish acrylic colours, the painting depicted a grey-haired grandmother sitting in a deckchair on a suburban lawn. The composition was bad and the drawing execrable.

Captain Midnight returned looking critical.

'Well, Babes,' he said, shaking his head in a puzzled way. 'You may call me Phil E. Stein. But in my humble opinion that is a piece of shit.'

'It is a piece of shit. Most of the stuff here is.'

'Which ones are yours?' Captain Midnight asked.

I pointed to a far wall where three of my paintings could be glimpsed through the chattering media folk. I had spent three months of the year living in France; and the paintings, a sort of offshoot of Abstract Impressionism, were an attempt to capture the light and colour of Provence. They didn't work the way I had originally hoped. But I wasn't entirely displeased with them.

'What were you smoking when you did them, Babes?' Captain Midnight asked, when he came back from a long examination of my work.

'Nothing. I was straight. I painted them in France. No dope at all. I even gave up alcohol.'

'Yeah? He looked at me with grudging admiration. 'If you paint that kind of stuff straight, your head must be in one helluva fucking mess. I thought you were going to tell me you were freaked out on mushrooms or something.'

'Fuck off.'

'Don't turn nasty on me, Stan. Remember I'm new at this culture crap. I might get into them after a while.'

His fingers began a light drumming on the trestle table. His head kept darting around. I recognized the signs and wasn't surprised when he suggested we leave.

'Where to?' I asked.

'Business discussion. I wish to employ your professional services.'

'You want a picture painted?'

'Nah. Your other professional services. Don't worry, the employment I offer is strictly legal. In no way does it involve certain substances.

'It doesn't?' I asked surprised.

'Absolutely not, my good man. Would you care to hear the fee I propose to offer you?'

'Alright. But I think it only fair to say that I am not interested. My instincts tell me that any offer of employment that comes through you can only end up in trouble. I have ignored my instincts on other occasions and regretted doing so.'

Captain Midnight smiled and nodded his head, making my twin images jump up and down in his glasses.

'Five hundred pounds,' he said. 'Cash. Half up-front.'

'Cash?'

'That is right.'

'Half up-front?'

'Right in your greedy grasping little palm.'

'Let's take a ride,' I said.

Eight

We drove through the night streets aimlessly, powered by a V8 engine and caprice. We headed towards no particular direction. There was no destination in mind. For Captain Midnight it was enough that we were once again moving, wheels hissing along the wet road surface, windscreen wipers clicking hypnotically. We were moving. Going no place and coming from nowhere. We existed only in the now. Here in this Ford Fairlane, being driven by a mad Zen master with gold fillings that kept catching the lamplight.

'That was pretty good grass,' I said to him, as I watched Sloane Square glide by.

'There's a bag of it in the glove compartment. And some skins. Why don't you roll us up one?'

I opened the glove compartment, found the bag and began rolling. Battersea Park went by. Then Clapham. We had a brief but exhilarating flirtation with East Putney, where Captain Midnight couldn't quite hold it all together for a few moments and drove the wrong way down a one-way system. When his brain came back from its temporary vacation, he drove on to Earl's Court.

We were making what I estimated to be our ninth and scariest trip along Park Lane when I felt compelled to question his fitness to drive.

'Don't worry, Babes. Captain Midnight is one ace driver. He has never had an accident.'

'Never?'

'Repeat, never. I've seen a lot of guys around me have accidents. But not me. You're safer with me than you are crossing a road.'

'Especially crossing a road in front of a car being driven by you.'

C. Midnight Esquire, as he sometimes styled himself in more

fanciful moments, set up a soft tuneless humming, presumably as an accompaniment to the music that was coming over the radio. He was several keys out, and his sense of rhythm was poor. His left shoulder began twitching in some strange dance, and he started making short ducking movements with his head. After a while, I worked out he was dancing.

'About this business you had for me,' I prompted, as I swiftly tired of his motions.

'Oh, yeah.' He stopped jerking around and became serious, sad even, as he reached into his jacket pocket.

He pulled out a brown envelope and handed it to me.

'It doesn't feel like there's two hundred and fifty quid here,' I said, holding the envelope between finger and thumb.

'There isn't. That's a photograph. Have a look at it.'

He pulled over and stopped under a streetlight.

'Doesn't the car run to an interior light?' I asked.

'Sure it does,' he said, offended. 'But I hate people peering in.'

I pulled a photograph out of the envelope. It was a colour polaroid and showed a young woman, with a funny, sharp-featured face and a mass of blonde curls, standing in front of a privet hedge. She was no beauty, but after a while the face began to grow on you.

'Who is she?' I asked.

'My old lady.'

I turned to stare into his dark glasses.

'Knock it off, Captain. You wouldn't get tied up with anything you couldn't put through a car-wash.'

Captain Midnight sighed and let in the clutch, making a sudden existential change of direction that had us going in a long skid for a moment or two.

'I am serious, Stan my good fellow,' he said solemnly, apparently unaffected by the sheer, stark terror we had just undergone while heading towards the plate-glass window of a supermarket.

'I believe you. Just slow down.'

He eased his foot off the accelerator as I rolled another joint to steady my nerves.

'This lady is my Numero Uno. The top of my personal charts.

She is the sunshine of my life. She puts a song in my heart and a shine on my soul. And she's got a pair of knockers that would cause a stampede in a monastery. I'd tell you how great she was in the sack, but I wouldn't want to see you consumed in the hard green flame of envy.'

I looked at the photograph again. The woman in it didn't seem to tally with Captain Midnight's claims. I would have thought her thin, if anything. And somehow she didn't look like a woman who would enjoy sex much. But it was hard to tell from a photograph. Especially just a polaroid snap.

We drove past the ugly mass of the BBC Television Centre. Captain Midnight lapsed into a sudden moroseness. When he slowed to allow an elderly couple a sporting chance of getting across a zebra crossing, I knew something was wrong.

'She's left me, Babes. Just took off and left,' he cried, stamping on the accelerator in a manner that had the elderly couple falling over the kerbstone as they scrambled to safety.

'Left you? You were living together? Where? In the boot?'

'Don't take the piss out of me, Stan. I'm suffering. Captain Midnight is not himself. His heart has been turned to Shredded Wheat. This chick is the very air he breathes. He is lost without her. That is why he wants you to help him. He wants you to find her.'

I shook my head.

'I don't take on that sort of thing. I'm not a real private eye. I just recover small quantities of dope when it goes missing.'

He turned to look at me, misjudged a corner and had us bumping heavily over a kerb.

'But I can relate to you, Babes,' he pleaded. 'I couldn't do that with a real private eye. Most of those guys are ex-pigs. I couldn't bare the innermost secrets of my soul to a former member of the filth. Five hundred big ones,' he tempted. 'You need the bread. Anita won't be back for a long while.'

'It isn't my sort of thing.'

'But I have so much confidence in you, my dear fellow.'

I thought about this proposition for a few moments.

'Two hundred and fifty up-front?' I checked.

'One hundred. Through your door, in an envelope tomorrow morning.'

'You said two hundred and fifty earlier.'

'That was just to grab your interest. The sort of thing advertising guys do. Legal, honest, decent and truthful. Almost. As a measure of my sincerity I'll make it a hundred and fifty. Through your letter-box by eleven. The rest to follow when Toorey is once again in my loving arms.'

'Toorey?' I questioned.

'You can't choose the name of the chick you fall in love with. It gets to sound okay after a while.'

'Maybe,' I conceded, thinking of her face. 'How about expenses?'

'You are stretching me over a barrel in my hour of need. Okay. But don't go charging for any lines of Charley you may have to snort up in pursuit of your enquiries.'

'I don't touch coke anymore,' I told him. 'It strips your defences. Are you serious about all this?'

'I am dying, Babes,' he sighed. 'Inside I am dying. Underneath all the flip remarks and the jokes, I am dying. Toorey really meant something to me. For the first time in my life. Ever.'

'Supposing I find her and she doesn't want to come back?'

Captain Midnight made a low moaning sound.

'Wowee. You really know how to twist that old knife in, don't you.' He took a resolute breath. 'Okay then. If she doesn't want to come back, I'll accept that. Painful as it may be. Just so long as I get to talk to her first. You just find where she is and let me go and talk to her first.'

I gave the matter my consideration as I stared at the walls of a bleak concrete underpass. A hundred and fifty wasn't a lot. But it would help, the way things were at the moment.

'Okay,' I agreed. 'Your hundred and fifty buys you two days. If I haven't found her after that, I still get to keep the money. As a gesture of goodwill, I'll include expenses in that sum.'

'You're a white man, Babes.'

I looked around my pockets until I came up with a pen and an old envelope.

'Okay,' I said, poised to write. 'Toorey what?'

'Toorey Dunphee. But that may not be her real name.'

'It's funny,' I said. 'I've only just started, but I feel this could turn out to be one of my more baffling cases.'

'She's a folk singer,' Captain Midnight explained, as I wrote the name down anyway. 'They often work under different names.'

'Where does she live?' I asked, pen poised again.

Captain Midnight paused while he gunned the car through a light that was just turning to red, then turned to me and shrugged.

'I don't know,' he said. 'Around Chalk Farm somewhere. I think there's a launderette on the corner. But I could be thinking of somewhere else.'

'I thought that she made it June in January for you? I thought that stars magically appeared when you spoke her name? The love of your life, and you don't even know where she lives?'

Captain Midnight chuckled in a self-deprecating way.

'Sounds crazy, doesn't it? I know. But I was so whacked out of my skull over this chick I never noticed where we were. I'd drop her home sometimes, but I was in no condition to register where she lived. I'm not into other people's places. You know that, Babes. I'm a freak. I admit it. My life takes place in this car. I've got everything I want here.' He gestured around the interior. 'You want a beer? There's one in an ice-box under the seat. Shave? There's an electric razor in the side-pocket on the door there. In the boot I've got a portable TV along with a few changes of threads. I press a button, and the driver's seat goes back into a bed.'

'Don't demonstrate it,' I cried as his seat began to tip back.

He pressed a button and the seat tipped upright again.

'I've got everything here,' he repeated.

'If you don't know where Toorey lives, how do you know she isn't at home now? Heartbroken because you haven't called?'

'She isn't at home. I talked to her agent. The guy who gets her work, singing around folk clubs. He doesn't know where she is. He's pissed off with her because she walked out halfway through a gig. I was supposed to meet her after that gig. At the Happy Mason in Woodchurch Road, over near Muswell Hill. When I got there, she'd already left. Done a super fast fade without saying a word to anyone. I was broken into a zillion pieces. That was a week ago. I haven't slept since.'

We paused at a set of lights, and I watched a half-hearted fistfight between two senior citizens exchanging slow-motion blows outside a brightly lit McDonald's. I didn't entirely believe Captain Midnight's story, I thought, still watching the oldsters circling each other. Then again it was all so unlikely that it might even be true. Whatever happened, I stood to make a hundred and fifty quid. It didn't really matter what Captain Midnight's true game was. I'd spend a couple of days looking for Toorey just hard enough to satisfy my conscience, and then I was out of it. Maybe I could use Captain Midnight's money to finance an expedition to Dumfries to find Anita.

'Alright then,' I agreed. 'I'll start off having a word with her agent. What's his name?'

'Paxton. Brian Paxton. He hangs out in Soho somewhere. He's in the book.'

'One hundred and fifty quid, through my door in the morning. By eleven. Right?'

Captain Midnight nodded solemnly.

'My word is my bond, my good fellow,' he assured me.

He stopped the car. To my surprise, we were outside my front door.

Nine

I was in bed by eleven and up again, cursing, at ten minutes past. Pulling on my blue and white Japanese robe, I went to look down out of the front window of my living room. There was a woman standing on my doorstep. I could see a plain black hat with matching shoes. There was a large briefcase under her arm. Trouble. The midnight knock of officialdom.

I let the blind fall back and went downstairs to open the front door.

'Yes?' I demanded sharply, as I looked at the woman.

'Mr Garland? Mr Stanley Garland?'

'Stan. Nobody ever calls me Stanley.'

'I think we'll make do with Mr Garland at the moment.'

She had dark auburn hair scraped back tightly under her hat, and the large, heavy-framed spectacles she wore were too heavy for her pert features. There was too much lipstick. A lot too much. And some of it had missed her lips by a good half inch. She looked a little crazy.

'I'm from the DHSS,' she announced. 'May we talk about this matter upstairs?'

'Isn't it a little late for you to be making your rounds?'

'You are never at home, Mr Garland. You leave us little choice. Believe me, I do not relish working these late hours. I would rather be at home sitting in front of a warm fire talking to my cat.'

'Okay,' I sighed. 'We might as well get it over with. But I'm sure there's been some mistake.'

'That, my dear Mr Garland, is what they all say.'

I let her in, closed the door and led the way upstairs. I offered to hang her raincoat on a hook in my narrow hallway, but the offer was declined with a curt shake of her head. Nor did she remove her hat or gloves. I took her into the living room.

'And you are?' I questioned, as I switched on a couple of sidelamps.

'Elaine Grant. Mizz Elaine Grant.'

I knelt to switch on an electric fire. It was cold enough for me to see my breath upon the air. I had a feeling it was going to be a long hard winter.

'Are there many of your fellow Americans working for the DHSS, Mizz Grant?' I asked, as the bars of the fire began to glow red.

'Not many, Mr Garland. Indeed, I believe I am the only one.'

She sat down on the only chair to open her briefcase and remove a sheaf of papers. As she crossed her legs, I caught a glimpse of pale white thighs, before the raincoat was swiftly pulled back into place. I offered coffee or tea, but she shook her head. From the Greek restaurant below, there came the sound of breaking crockery. A party probably.

My visitor tapped a pen against her clumsily painted lips and looked at me thoughtfully through her heavy, black-framed spectacles. I courteously angled the electric fire more towards her.

'Some of the questions I ask may seem a trifle strange,' she began. 'Bizarre even. But I can assure you the information is necessary for our files.'

'Supposing I don't care to answer these questions of yours?'

She frowned at me.

'Please don't adopt a truculent attitude, Mister Garland. It will do you no good in the end. I have considerable powers of authority to back me up. It will be in your own interests to adopt a more co-operative manner.'

'Alright,' I said. 'Let's hear one of your questions.'

'Very well.' She bent her head over the sheaf of papers. 'Do you live alone, Mr Garland?'

'Most of the time.'

'Would you care to clarify that statement?'

'Most of the time I live alone. But on rare occasions I cohabit.'

'I see.' She made a note with her pen, then looked up at me again. 'This cohabiting. Does it take place with males or females?'

'Females exclusively.'

She scribbled another note on her pad.

'This cohabiting. Of what duration is it normally? A year? A month? A week? A couple of hours?'

'It's hard to say. They vary considerably.'

'I shall put NFP if that's alright with you. No Fixed Period. That should cover it. Now these females you cohabit exclusively with. You screw them, I take it?'

'Well, usually. Yes.'

I became aware that part of my Japanese robe had slipped away, exposing my naked genitals to Mizz Grant's critical stare. I pulled the robe back into place.

'And how would you rate your sexual ability?' she continued. 'Average? Below average? Middling to fair? Accomplished? Very good? Excellent? Which category would you place yourself in?'

'That's difficult. I think you'd better put NFP again. No Fixed Performance.'

Mizz Grant stood up.

'That won't do, I'm afraid,' she said, sternly. 'I must have the exact and precise information.'

Watching me closely, she slowly undid the buttons of her raincoat. She was naked beneath it.

'Why Mizz Grant,' I said. 'Without your raincoat, you're beautiful.'

'I have no time for flippancy, Mister Garland,' she chided, unsmilingly. 'I have a very full schedule. Where is your bedroom, please? I shall have to do this rating myself. This is one of the things I can't trust to a computer.'

Later, when we were lying in bed together, untangling the sheets, I complimented her.

'Pretty good,' I said. 'But I think the stuff about sitting in front of a warm fire talking to your cat was a bit over the top. And the lipstick's a bit overdone.'

'You asshole,' she said angrily. 'I spend three hours getting into character, freezing my ass off in the cold out there, and all you can say is it was a bit over the top. Jeezus.'

Maggie Spizer swung her legs out of the bed, stood up and looked down at me, getting angrier by the minute. Once, many years ago back in her native New York City, Maggie had done a course of method acting with Lee Strasberg. She was very serious about acting. If the commercial she auditioned for called for a housewife, Maggie would turn up with a mop, a bucket, a borrowed child and a complete set of motivations. Should some avant-garde pantomime director suddenly decide that Long John Silver must be played by a woman, I was sure that Maggie would turn up for the audition with one of her legs amputated.

Maggie didn't get a lot of work, but her persistence was admirable. She kept the faith with Lee's training by employing it in her sex life. During the three or so months of our relationship, I had opened the door to a district nurse, a traffic-warden, an imperious policewoman and a nun whose language had succeded in making me blush.

There had been others. A frigid English nanny with crotchless knickers and the worst accent I had ever heard, a Thomas Hardy country maiden who sounded as if she came from Dorset via Chattanooga, a depraved schoolgirl who employed a hockey stick in a manner that would have raised eyebrows at Roedean. And more. Many more.

The more successful creations paid return visits. But not the nun. I was happy about that. It was the nun who had come closest to shocking me with both her language and her demands. During her visit, I was constantly waiting for a bolt of lightning to smash through my bedroom window and blast us both to the Hell which, as a sort of Buddhist, I didn't believe in.

'Where did you leave your clothes?' I asked, watching her light a cigarette. A habit I strongly disapprove of, after kicking a three pack a day habit myself.

'In the car, asshole. Where do you think?'

She blew a cloud of smoke in my direction, knowing I didn't like it.

'Is it too late to say that I think talking to the cat was a terrific character touch? And I'm coming around to the lipstick as well.'

'Blow it out your ass, Stan Garland.'

'Honest. The cat was a really nice touch. It was the key to the whole character. A subtle definition of her wants and needs.'

She carried on blowing smoke in my direction. But her expression had softened a little.

'Yeah?'

'Really.'

'Did it make you horny?'

'Yes. So did the gloves. That was a nice touch, keeping them on.'

Maggie shook her head in wonderment.

'You English are so fucking decadent,' she said, as she covered herself with my Japanese robe. 'No wonder you lost your Empire and all your loot. You were all too busy jerking each other off in your leather bondage outfits. Did you know it was me at first?'

'No,' I lied. 'Not until you started in with the questionnaire.'

'Asshole,' she snapped, suddenly angry again. 'You always have to go and overdo it. I can tell when you're lying. Shit. I worked really hard on that character. I went and hung around the DHSS for almost two weeks solid. How did you recognise me?'

'You were chewing gum. You always chew gum. Even the nun chewed gum.'

Maggie smiled in an evil mocking way.

'She really shook you up every which way but loose, that little old nun, didn't she? I think she might have to come calling again, real soon.'

'No,' I protested quickly. 'It's sort of against my religious beliefs.'

Maggie bent over and reached for me under the bedclothes.

'Well, well, what have we got here?' She asked, in a pretty good W.C. Fields voice. 'A stirring down in the forest.' She chuckled triumphantly and then, in her own voice, said, 'That red corselette was a nice touch, huh? That babe with the habit, knows how to grab it where it counts, don't she?'

She ground her cigarette out in an ashtray she had brought in from the living room, then came back into bed.

She pulled back the sheet and looked down between my legs.

'Well, hello there, big boy,' she said, in a Mae West voice. 'Is that a Cruise missile between your legs or are you just pleased to see me?'

Lowering her head she took me into her mouth. She was still chewing gum. I felt as if my member was being sucked into a meat-grinder.

'Stop,' I cried out. 'Stop. You're killing me.'

Maggie lifted her head and looked at me.

'You serious?' she asked. 'Or are you getting off on some fantasy?'

'I'm serious. It was like being given a blow-job by Jaws.'

Maggie shrugged, making her small, pert breasts jiggle around.

'Well, I was still pissed off with you. I guess there was some latent hostility coming through. It was good for me that I was able to release it. Doctor Werner says, I must never hold my hostility in. I should always let go of it.'

A decade or so earlier, I had spent three years in Philadelphia at an obscure college founded by a man who had made a fortune out of canning vegetables. Proud of some distant British connection, he had made an art scholarship available to those born in the British Isles, and I had been steered onto it by an American friend. I turned out to be only the fourth Brit to take up the founder's kind offer since its inception in 1911.

I didn't add a lot to my knowledge of art in those years, but I learned a lot about American women, and about the sacrosanct nature of their relationship with their psychiatrists. You didn't make jokes about people like Doctor Werner. It was a hostile and aggressive thing to do, implying all sorts of knots and tangles in your own psyche. I had destroyed many a beautiful and meaningful relationship by taking the piss out of smartasses like Doctor Werner.

'How is the Good Doctor?' I asked. 'Still stashing it away in her numbered Swiss bank account?'

Maggie lit another cigarette. It was a deliberately provocative act – knowing, as she did, how I felt about tobacco smoke in the bedroom. It played havoc with my Qigong breathing exercises in the mornings.

'She says I ought to give you the old heave-ho,' Maggie said.

'She does, eh?'

'You're a very non-constructive person to have a relationship with. You're a fuck-up. Doctor Werner thinks you need professional help.'

I moved away sharply.

'Mind where you're flicking that ash,' I said. 'I'm still feeling sensitive.'

'A lot of guys would like it, I'll bet. You English are so kinky I bet I could find guys who'd pay me to do it to them.'

'Maybe. Why don't you save the idea up for your next session with Doctor Werner? She can probably come up with a few juicy case histories.'

I climbed out of bed, went out to the kitchen and returned with a glass of water.

'For a sort of Buddhist you get very hostile sometimes,' Maggie said, as I came back. 'You're a very contracted sort of person. Tight. Unwilling to grow. Maybe Doctor Werner's right about giving you the old heave-ho. I think you could be stunting my personal growth. I worked out all my hostility a long time ago. I don't need to hang around with a guy who's still into all that shit.'

She sat smoking, flicking ash in all directions as she watched me through a cloud of tobacco smoke. She was still chewing gum.

'Didn't you used to be an alcoholic?' she asked, watching me sip my water.

'No. I was a heavy drinker. But I wasn't an alcoholic. I got drunk most nights. Not falling-down drunk. But just enough to wake up with a slight hangover the next mornings. I only drank wine. But I had to buy a bottle every night without fail. That's what got to me in the end. The predictability. I hate to be dependent on anything. I gave up cigarettes six years ago for the same reason.'

'But you smoke dope,' Maggie pointed out. 'That's a dependency. A crutch.'

'Not for me. I can take it or leave it alone. I don't have to have it like I did booze. If it's there, fine. If it isn't, that's alright too.'

'Booze, cigarettes. Are you going to give up sex, too?'

I took another sip of water, wishing momentarily it was a chilled Chablis.

'I don't know,' I said. 'It is, after all, only another dependency, another need to be satisfied. The Buddha said the end of desire is the end of unhappiness.'

'The end of desire for a guy is when his cock drops off or they lower him into the earth,' Maggie stated.

'What about women? You seem quite keen on sex yourself.'

'Sure. Doctor Werner thinks sex is very important to me. She's very interested in these role-playing fantasies I've been working on with you. She may even write a paper on them. Isn't that something? Little Maggie Spizer from 98th and Riverside makes an important contribution to psychiatry.'

'If she publishes one word, I'll sue.'

'Don't be a dummy,' Maggie said, laughing. 'She won't use our real names. 'It'll be Maggie Y and Stan X. Come on, you can't stand there without any clothes on looking angry. It doesn't work with a limp dick.'

'I'm not angry,' I said angrily.

'You shouldn't be. You'll be pleased and flattered when you read her paper. I grossly exaggerated your measurements. Doctor Werner gets off on that sort of thing.'

Ten

I was awake at six the next morning and very soon in the living room to perform my routine of exercises and breathing. I was onto my Tai Chi by the time Maggie showed herself around the door. I skipped my meditation and had breakfast with her. She approved of the sesame spread, but insisted on mixing it with marmalade on her own slice of wholewheat toast. It made me realise once again the many basic incompatibilities we have with the inhabitants of the US of A.

When Maggie left for an audition at some fringe theatre, I walked along to Camden Town tube station and caught the tube to Tottenham Court Road.

I found Brian Paxton's agency on the second floor of a seedy, dark building halfway along a narrow alley running off Wardour Street. There was a sandwich bar next door, and I stopped to live dangerously with the caffeine from a cup of non-freerange coffee. It was only a few minutes after ten, but the staff were already preparing for the lunchtime rush, buttering stacks of sliced bread and adding assorted fillings. One fat, bald man with a large straggly moustache sang loudly along with the radio. Every now and then he would break off singing to engage in some banter with an unseen figure on the other side of the serving hatch. I couldn't follow the language the banter was conducted in, but the fat man kept winking in my direction, graciously including me in the general camaraderie.

He was still laughing when I reached the cash register to pay. And he continued to laugh as I gathered my change, pulled on my raincoat and opened the door to the street.

When I got outside, I found he had overcharged me by some thirty pee.

Not wishing to risk the ancient lift, I climbed the stairs to Brian Paxton's office, passing an import-export business that seemed to have hit hard times and what I took to be the 'model' from the third floor. The 'model' wore a tight black leather skirt and long shiny black boots. Her make-up could have been applied by Rouault. For a moment I thought it was Maggie up to her tricks again and I had the beginnings of an erection.

I paused when I got to Brian Paxton's landing, breathing heavily and wondering if the thudding of my heart came from the sight of the model's black leather skirt or from my poor condition. I resolved to increase my exercise and breathing programme by a further half-hour each morning. When everything was more or less back in working order, I pushed open the door of Brian Paxton's office.

An ageing flower child was making toast over the single bar of an electric fire. Long mousy hair fell to the waistband of her patterned dirndl skirt. As she stood up, breasts that may once have launched a thousand love-ins sagged towards a thickening waist. She stood up with an agility belied by her appearance.

'Yes?' she asked, still holding the slice of bread fixed to the point of the knife. 'Can I help you?'

'Brian Paxton. Is he in? I'd like to see him for a few moments.'

She looked me over.

'Are you an act?' she asked doubtfully.

The nails on the hand that held the knife were broken and dirty.

'I'm not an act. I'm for real,' I said.

There was a straw shopping basket on her desk. In it there was a box of man-size Kleenex, a pair of slippers and a copy of 'The Prophet'. She probably wore granny glasses to read it.

'You're not official, are you?' she asked. 'Tax or something?'

'In these clothes?' I asked, offended, gesturing at my white shoes, jeans and the yellow leather jacket that had cost me £150 in a sale.

She shrugged, unimpressed. Her breasts stirred like large sleeping dogs.

'Most officials are corrupt,' she said. 'The very nature of their jobs makes them prone to corruption. They're only human, I suppose. They want to drive fast cars and wear flashy clothes –'

'Flashy?' I protested.

'That yellow plastic jacket you've got on is flashy.'

'This isn't plastic. It's leather. I paid a hundred and fifty quid for it in a half price sale.'

She shrugged her heavy-looking shoulders.

'Well, it looks cheap and nasty,' she said.

'You make me sound like a double act.'

A look of realization came over her face.

'Oh, is that what you are?' she said. 'I should have known. In those clothes. You're a comic turn. I don't know if Mr Paxton is taking on any more comic turns at the moment. There's something of a glut. Everyone seems to be going for alternative comedians right now. You'd be too old for that. Alternative comedians are usually around thirty.'

'Do I get to see Brian Paxton?' I asked edgily.

'What about?'

'One of his clients. Toorey Dunphee.'

She hesitated for a moment, looking a little worried.

'Do you want to book her?' she asked.

'Is she available?'

'She's got a very full engagement book at the moment,' she claimed, still looking worried. 'She's very popular.'

'Not with the guy who runs the folk club above the Happy Mason, she isn't.'

'Just what do you want?' she asked irritably.

'The same thing as I did when I came in here. I'd like to see Brian Paxton for a few moments. It's no big deal.'

'I don't think he'll want to see you,' she said like a large sulky child. 'He doesn't like your sort of person.'

I sat down on the edge of her desk.

'Why don't you go and ask him,' I suggested. 'Then we'll both know for sure.'

She hesitated for a moment. Then she went over to a door leading to another office. When she had slammed the door behind her, I picked up the toast, spread it with some sunflower margarine I found and began to eat it. I could hear voices coming from the other room, but indistinctly. Nothing I could make any sense out of. I had just finished the toast when the door opened again. I guiltily brushed crumbs from my mouth.

51

'You can go in,' the ageing flower child said, openly hostile.

'Peace and love and may your Crosby, Stills and Nash albums never wear out,' I blessed her, as I passed.

Brian Paxton was an ancient old hippy. Bald on top, he had let his remaining hair grow down to his shoulders. He had a beard too, grey like his hair but yellowed with nicotine around the chin area. His thin body was clad in a pair of acid-green cords that made me glad I didn't inflict hangovers on myself anymore, and the sort of baggy, shapeless sweater other men might have saved for a camping holiday in the Lake District.

He moved across from a window that hadn't seen a cleaner in a long while, extending a long, limp hand. Clasping the hand was like taking hold of a dead bird.

'Don't mind Linda,' he apologized as the door slammed shut behind me. 'She's very protective towards me. I bring out the mother in her.' He flashed a smile I didn't immediately take to. 'You're not from the tax people, are you? Not in that clobber. Linda thought you might be VAT.'

'I wanted to ask you about Toorey Dunphee.'

Brian Paxton frowned.

'Not a very popular name around here at the moment,' he said.

He moved away from me to sit down behind his desk, lowering the acid green cords onto a swivel chair. Behind him, the wall was lined with photographs of smiling showfolk. Many of the men wore tuxedos, and nearly all the women exposed generous amounts of fishnet tights. There was also a mind-reading act that stared back at me with fixed, grim expressions. Maybe they had just seen the downward spiral of their inseparable career as the photograph was being taken. It was my guess that signing up with Brian Paxton could only have hastened that descent.

I declined Paxton's offer of a seat, not wishing to occupy a chair that was at least a foot lower than his own. Maybe his clients found it reassuring to have him looking down at them. But I knew it would just have pissed me off.

'May I ask why you want to ask me about Toorey Dunphee?' he asked, resting his elbows on his desk and pressing the tips of his fingers together.

'She's walked out on her boyfriend. I'm trying to find her for him.'

'Goodness,' he said, with a thrilled shudder. 'Are you a private detective? How glamorous.'

'I'm not anything like that. I'm just doing a favour for a friend. A sort of friend,' I added.

Brian Paxton held his head on one side to look at me in a quizzical way. The grey hair fell aside to reveal a small crucifix swinging from his earlobe. 'You don't look like one of Pete's friends,' he said, at last.

'Pete?'

'Your sort of friend. Toorey's boyfriend.'

There was a sudden aggressive burst of typing from next door as Linda worked off some of her hostility. She had probably worked out where her toast had gone.

'What does Pete look like?' I asked.

Brian Paxton shook his head gently, making the crucifix swing again.

'He's your sort of friend. You tell me what he looks like.'

I described Captain Midnight. As near as it was humanly possible to do so.

'No,' Brian Paxton said decisively. 'Nothing like Pete. Pete is shortish, blond and very muscular. The hair is dyed, but the muscles are real. He works out with weights. Quite good-looking. A sort of down-market Adonis. Don't tell him I said that or he'll probably come and do something brutal to me.'

He shuddered in a way that suggested he didn't find the idea entirely unpleasant.

'Maybe you talked to my friend on the phone. He says he talked to you about her.'

'Possibly. I can't recall. I talk to so many people on the phone. A lot of people have been ringing to ask me where Toorey is.'

'And what do you tell them?'

He raised his hands in a despairing gesture that would probably have won him an award at a French sidewalk cafe.

'Nothing,' he said. 'There's nothing to tell. She's vanished. She took off without finishing her set at the Happy Mason. I've had to cancel half a dozen other bookings since. It isn't going to do her career any good at all. Not at this stage. I was hoping to move her on from the folk club circuit. I've got a couple of telly people interested. At least, I did have.'

'You've no idea why she suddenly vanished? Or why?'

'None. If you were a real private detective, I would consider hiring you myself. Her vanishing act is going to cost me money, apart from all the time I've invested in her. I really am very cross with her.'

I reached into my pocket, took out the photograph Captain Midnight had given me and handed it to him.

'This is Toorey Dunphee, isn't it?' I asked.

He took the photograph and looked at it under his desk lamp with the aid of a pair of gold-rimmed glasses hanging from a chain around his neck.

'It's not a very good picture. But that's her alright. She can look much better than that in a professional shot. She's no beauty. But her face sort of grows on you after a while.'

'What about Pete?' I asked, as he returned the photograph to me. 'Doesn't he have any idea where she is?'

Brian Paxton offered me a cigarette from a packet of Gitanes. I declined. He took one out for himself and lit it with a stick lighter.

'Pete has vanished too,' he said, letting smoke out of his mouth.

'Ah,' I said for no particular reason.

'He swings both ways, you know,' Paxton told me spitefully. 'He is quite good-looking – if you like that sort of thing.' He looked at me questioningly.

'I don't,' I said. 'I swing strictly towards members of the opposite sex. Just the one way.'

'Oh, you poor soul,' he commiserated. 'You miss out on so much. I just love being bisexual. It's a gift from God.'

The door opened as the help came in to place a cup of tea in front of her employer, pointedly ignoring any requirements I might have had. She banged the door again on the way out.

'Would you like some tea?' Paxton asked.

'I wouldn't want to risk swallowing what Linda might put in it.'

He took a sip from the cup and grimaced.

'You're not missing much,' he said. 'Linda isn't much in the catering department.'

'But she is always okay for making up a threesome, should some tiresome person drop out, I take it?'

'I've no idea,' he said, with a little laugh. 'I shouldn't think so. I don't think Linda has a sex life. She's devoted her life to alternative religion. The Friends of the Inner Light. Do you know them?'

'I think I've seen their ads in Time Out. I keep meaning to go along and have a look. I'm a bit of an alternative religion buff myself.'

'Oh, I shouldn't think you'd like this lot. Not a lot of fun, I'm afraid. The woman who runs them is completely crazy. Hates sex in any form. All her followers have to become celibate. And people pay her money to join. Quite a lot, I believe. Astonishing, isn't it?'

'Maybe it's some new perversion. Paying not to get laid. It's the sort of thing that could catch on in America.'

I leaned against a wall, resting my foot on a camera case that stood next to some studio lights stacked in one corner.

'Careful,' Brian Paxton cautioned. 'That stuff costs a fortune. I do clients' photographs for them sometimes. The fees that professional photographers charge can cripple someone just starting out.'

'Do you think Pete and Toorey went off together?' I asked.

He shrugged, bringing his narrow shoulders up in line with his ears before dropping them again.

'It's possible. I don't know when Pete took off. I only heard that he disappeared, from someone or other. You could try asking at the place the Friends of the Inner Light have. Pete works there as a sort of handyman. They give him a room rent free in return. God knows why. He's hardly the spiritual type. Linda hates him.'

'Alternative religion doesn't seem to have done a lot for Linda's feelings of compassion and goodwill towards her fellow men.'

The buzzer on the office phone went. Paxton picked up the receiver and spent the next five minutes booking a comedy conjuring act for a week at a motel in East Anglia. I didn't think the act was going to be very pleased with the fee he finally agreed to take.

'I thought agents were supposed to be good at bargaining,' I said, as he put the phone back.

'It's November,' he explained. 'Not a good time of the year for those of my temperament. I need sunshine and light to operate properly. Today is one of my especially low days. I usually stay away from the office when I feel like this. But the kids are home from school. I didn't think I could handle all that noise and energy. Not today. Do you have kids?'

'No.'

'Oh, I love kids,' he enthused. 'Kids are wonderful. I adore them. If men could give birth to kids, I'd be the happiest person in the whole world.'

'Maybe science will have worked something out by the time you come around again for your next life,' I said.

Paxton sighed as he jabbed his cigarette out in an ashtray.

'I'll probably come back as a raging heterosexual,' he said sadly. 'Knowing my luck. If you do find Toorey, tell her to get in touch with me immediately.'

'I'll do that. If I see her.'

I'd got as far as the door when his voice stopped me.

'I don't want to appear rude. But I've got to ask. Where did you get that kinky plastic jacket? It's gorgeous.'

Linda didn't look up as I came out into the room. Her head remained bent over the office typewriter, as her blunt fingers, with their unpolished nails, jabbed inexpertly at the keys. I thought about asking her for the address of the Friends of the Inner Light, but decided against it. As I stepped out onto the landing, the phone rang. She answered it in a voice near to sobbing. Unrequited love for Brian Paxton or the loss of her toast, I thought.

Walking down the stairs towards the streets, I began to experience a sudden wave of irrational sadness myself. Paxton was right. November was that kind of month.

Eleven

There was an envelope in my letter box when I got home. C. Midnight Esquire had kept his word. I checked to make sure the £150 was all there and then went on upstairs to make myself some lunch. There were bean sprouts in the fridge and half a packet of vegetarian rissole mix in the cupboard. What more could a man want? When I had the rissoles under the grill, I poured a glass of grape juice, swallowed a couple of ginseng capsules, then fiddled around with the portable radio until I found some Erik Satie.

As I sipped at the grape juice, I wondered what Captain Midnight was up to. Not that it mattered much. I only owed him another day of my time after this one. Part of me – my romantic side – still thought it just possible his tale of lost love was true. Just. But my instincts told me he was up to something devious. I was almost tempted to keep the money and do nothing. But some puritan work ethic principle wouldn't let me do that. Besides, it would be dishonest. As a sort of Buddhist, I had no time for dishonesty.

I was speculating about pouring soy sauce over my vegetarian rissoles when the phone rang. It was Judd Gleason from the gallery to say one of my paintings had been sold. He sounded pleased and soon rang off. If Captain Midnight's story was true, he needed the money even more than I did. After a few mental calculations, I worked out that I would end up with something like forty quid by the time I had paid the gallery commission and my framing bill, plus the cost of the canvas, paints, etcetera.

Depressed by my calculations and bitter at the many injustices inflicted on practitioners of the arts, I poured too much soy sauce over my rissoles and rendered them inedible. I pecked moodily at a couple of bean shoots, then gave up all thought of eating and filled my water pipe with hash.

I smoked for a while, then went and looked out of the window. The weather had taken a turn for the worse. The sun that had warmed the morning had been chased away by a rain-laden wind that had the passers-by hunched deep down in their coats. The sky was a uniform grey. Only two-thirty still, but it was already growing dark. There were lights on in the windows of the block of flats opposite. Directly across from me an old man, with a dark woollen dressing gown pulled around his throat, stared into my window. When I began to wonder seriously if he might be a member of the drug squad on a stake-out, I realised that the hash had made me paranoid in the way it did on rare occasions. Usually when I was prone to being depressed, like now.

Moving away from the window, I went over to my record collection, but everything seemed familiar and dull. Even a quick burst of bluegrass from Flatt and Scruggs failed to cheer me up. I felt a nasty bout of *Weltschmerz* coming on.

By four I knew I had to get out of the house. It was either that or slash my wrists with an electric razor. Calling upon awesome reserves of will-power, I lifted the telephone directory and looked up the address of the Friends of the Inner Light. Summoning even more will-power, I replaced the directory, put my raincoat on and stumbled downstairs towards my car. When the engine finally caught, I drove towards Kentish Town.

It was raining heavily by the time I found a parking space between two of the many Volvo estates lining either side of Gilmour Street. The street was on the way up, judging by the business that Habitat was evidently doing in the area. My lips were curling into a sneer when I spotted several roller-blinds identical in design to the ones I had for my own living-room windows.

No. 32 was a pleasantly decaying semi-detached, built in richly coloured old brick. Rainwater gushed from a piece of broken, hanging guttering, to run down the brick and form a muddy pool across the cracked concrete path. There were weeds pushing through the cracks. On either side of the path, there was scrubby grass dotted with dog turds. The paint on the front door was peeling. The bell didn't look as though it would work, but I pushed it anyway. I was about to resort to the rusting knocker when the door opened, emitting a strong smell of incense.

'Hello.'

The greeting was friendly, if limp and came from a small, thin man with a straggly beard. The beard, like his receding hair, was grey. The shapeless, baggy cardigan and flannel trousers he wore were also grey. His skin was a paler variation of the same colour. His nylon shirt was blue. But it was a blue that was edging towards grey, speeded along by not being washed in a long time.

'Hello,' I returned, with an open, honest smile. 'I wonder if you could help me?'

I caught sight of my smile reflected in a mirror somewhere behind him. I recalled seeing the smile before somewhere. On a face other than my own. But neither the face nor the name of its owner would come to mind.

'It's possible,' the bearded little fellow said. 'We do manage to help many people. There are many paths to the Inner Light, perhaps we can help you find your own particular one. Indeed, you might have already placed your foot upon your own path by coming here.' He stood aside, motioning for me to enter. 'Isn't this rain terrible?' he commented in a more prosaic tone.

'The rain is just rain,' I rebuked him, irritated by his smugness and clobbering him with a little Zen. 'It is neither good or bad. It simply is. You shouldn't impose your own prejudices on it.'

'I don't have prejudices,' he countered. 'Not anymore. This way, please.'

Passing the mirror, I tried out my smile again. I remembered where I had seen it before – Richard Nixon.

He led me into a small room furnished with a desk and a few chairs. Behind the desk was a window with a view of spiky, leafless trees and the back windows of the houses opposite. The walls of the room were painted white. But that had probably been a long time ago, and the white had taken on a yellowish tinge. There were phtographs pinned to a couple of large cork boards mounted on one of the walls. As the man bent to fiddle with an electric fan heater, I looked at them.

Linda, the ageing hippy woman from Paxton's office, looked

back at me. She was one of a group, most of them mature, performing Tai Chi movements. A yang style, I noted professionally from the large exaggerated postures the performers were frozen in. I practise a yin form, where the movements and stances are smaller. As the little fellow messing around with the fan heater had said, there are many paths to the Inner Light. Linda's stance wasn't bad. But I thought that the 'Snoopy' tee-shirt was a little young for the large, mature knockers it was doing its best to cover.

I found Linda in another photograph. She was wearing a plain tee-shirt with her jogging trousers this time. Her eyes were closed, as she sat in a cross-legged position along with a group of fellow meditators. Far from beaming with inner peace, she looked as if she was pissed off about something. I couldn't find her in any of the other pictures, although there was a rear view that could have been hers, in a circle performing what looked like some kind of psychodrama.

'Who's this?' I asked, pointed to a large blown-up portrait of a middle-aged woman with a lot of frizzy white hair and large, crazy-looking eyes.

'Ruth Armstrong,' the man said, seeming surprised by my ignorance. 'The founder and leader of the Friends.'

He stood up, walked behind the desk and sat down. I turned away from the photographs and took the chair he indicated. Rain pounded against the window as the sky turned darker.

'What is your problem?' he asked.

'Problem?'

'Everybody who comes to us has a problem of some kind.' He gave a soft, annoying chuckle. 'Oh, you are not unique, my friend. Whatever your problem is you may rest assured there are others with the same one. And many with far greater problems. Does it bother you not to be unique? Does your ego feel threatened?'

He leaned back in the chair, with a patronizing expression on his face, waiting for me to rise to the bait. I had seen the same, smug, self-satisfied look on the face of a hypnotherapist I had once visited in my constant search for self-improvement. On the second visit I had been so incensed by the hypnotherapist's sneering criticism that I had taken hold of him by the shirt collar and threatened him with physical violence. But that had been many years ago. I was a little further along now. A little.

'When you find the Inner Light, all your problems will disappear,' the smug little asshole continued. 'Your way will suddenly be clear. The darkness will be dispelled.'

'I bet it doesn't come cheap,' I said.

He shrugged dismissively.

'What is money?' he asked.

I echoed both the tone and the shrug.

'What is an overdraft?' I asked back. 'What is an Income Tax demand?'

His manner hardened up a little.

'I'm not entirely sure of why you have come here. What is it you want of us, friend?'

'I wanted to ask about Pete.'

'Pete?'

'Your live-in handyman.'

'Ah, Pete.' He nodded. 'A restless spirit, I'm afraid. Are you a friend of his?'

I shrugged.

'What is a friend?' I questioned, in his style.

'Pete left here,' he said flatly.

'When? In earthly terms?'

'Oh, I don't know,' he said, without a lot of interest. 'A week or so. I'm not very good on time, I'm afraid.'

His concentration was suddenly taken up with the movements of some small insect crossing his desk. Just as the insect reached the far edge, he picked up a ruler, squashed the creature then scraped it off into a metal waste-paper bin.

'Aren't you concerned about the bad karma incurred by the taking of a life?' I said.

He smiled as he shook his head.

'No,' he said unworried. 'It was an unclean, lowly creature. I showed my love for it by killing it and hastening its rebirth into a higher form of existence. I killed with love.'

'Have you any idea where Pete went to?'

'None. To be perfectly honest I didn't like him very much. I was glad when he left. His vibrations were not harmonious. Ruth is over-charitable sometimes, I feel. Pure herself, she is slow to see the evil in others. Pete is not a good person. I don't think he even wants to be. He has served time in prison, you know.'

'I didn't,' I said, beginning to wonder once again about Captain Midnight's tale of unrequited love.

'Breaking into chemist shops, that sort of thing. He was addicted to heroin. Ruth took him on from one of those halfway house places they have for former addicts who have been cured. If that's possible. I think Pete was still addicted.'

The window rattled as a gust of rain and wind battered at it. The lights dimmed momentarily. I was beginning to find the whole place somewhat spooky.

'Why did you think Pete was still addicted?' I asked.

'I'm a very aware person. Sometimes I think I can read minds. I sensed lots of bad things about Pete. Drug abuse was just one of many things I felt about him. Also –' He leaned forward. 'I once smelled hashish coming from his room.'

'How did you know it was hashish?'

'In my student days I attended several parties where people were smoking it. Not that I indulged myself.'

'Hash isn't heroin.'

'One thing leads quickly to another. Anger to violence, desire to lust, sensuality to depravity. The temporal pleasures of the flesh all lead to unhappiness. That was another thing about Pete. He had women in his room. Or a woman, at least.'

'Go on. The mind boggles.'

'You don't understand. Celibacy is one of our vows. Spiritual progression is impossible while the mind is still taken up with sex.'

On impulse I took the photograph of Toorey out of my pocket.

'Did you ever see this woman he had in his room?' I asked.

'I caught a glimpse of her on a couple of occasions.'

'Was this her?' I asked, showing him the photograph of Toorey.

He examined it closely under the desk light.

'It could be. Yes, I believe it was. Just what is going on? Are you some kind of detective?'

'I thought you would have been able to vibe that out with your amazing awareness and insight.'

'You're not a detective,' he stated.

'Very good. Maybe I'll sign up for one of your courses, after all.'

I stood up.

'I don't think you're our sort of person,' he said.

I reached over and took the photograph from him.

'Probably not,' I agreed. 'To be frank, I'm not happy about your attitude to wood-lice.'

I left him sitting at the desk and went out into the hall. I had just got as far as the front door when the doorbell rang. Linda, the ageing hippy woman, was standing on the doorstep, her long greying hair flattened with rain.

'What are you doing here?' she demanded.

'I'm looking for Pete.'

'But you were looking for Toorey when you came to the office this morning.'

'I still am. But now I'm looking for Pete as well.'

'Why?'

I took a chance on what I guessed to be her attitude towards the male species in general.

'Well, you know how it is,' I said. 'He got this girl into trouble and left her in the lurch. And now she's penniless.'

'Typical. There's a baby, is there?'

'Triplets,' I said, immediately cursing my tendency towards exaggeration. 'The girl was the daughter of a feminist activist doing time for assaulting the police at a rally,' I heard myself invent, with disbelief.

'Bastards. The police are all bastards. Men are all bastards. Pete's a real sod.'

'Yes?' I prompted. But she seemed disinclined to elaborate.

'What are you, then?' she asked. 'Some kind of private detective? They're all bastards, too,' she stated, without waiting for my reply.

'Do you have any idea where I might find Pete?'

'The same place as Toorey probably. Though God knows what they see in each other. I don't know where they've gone. To tell you the truth, I don't care either.'

When I left, she was standing in front of the hall mirror, angrily brushing rain from her hair. It probably wasn't fair to judge on meeting just two of its members – but from what I could see, the Friends of the Inner Light didn't seem big on love and compassion towards their fellow creatures.

Twelve

With a couple of hours to kill before I could go over to the Happy Mason, I left my car where it was and went to a pub a little way down the street. By chance I fell into conversation with an investigative journalist for one of the more moronic tabloids who lived locally. He had once gathered information for an article on the Friends of the Inner Light, but had been unable to come up with anything other than the standard 'bunch of nutters pissing about with the occult' stuff, and his editor had killed the story.

'They're probably harmless,' he admitted with a certain professional reluctance, as he sipped at the scotch and water I had bought him.

He was a heavy, red-faced man, with dark, greasy hair that kept falling in front of his eyes. His shirt collar was frayed and there was a shine on his cheap blue serge suit. His breath would have floored a gorilla.

'I wouldn't mind knowing where they get their money from though,' he said. 'They must have a few bob. This isn't a cheap area anymore.'

'They don't look as if they're doing very well – judging by the state of the place.'

I took a swallow of my tonic water and orange juice.

'There's something fishy going on there somewhere,' he said, through a mouthful of peanuts.

'Maybe that's just wishful thinking.'

'Wishful thinking, bollocks. If I'd had another couple of weeks on the story, I'd have come up with something.'

'You said they were probably harmless a few moments ago.'

'I know, I know. But deep down I have this feeling. You develop an instinct for that sort of thing in my business.'

'That's because you're an aware person. Do you ever think you can read minds?'

He looked up surprised, shifting around on his bar stool to look at me more closely.

'Do you know, I do sometimes,' he said. 'It sounds barmy. But sometimes I really think I can.'

He pushed his empty glass into my line of vision. I signalled the barman and ordered another scotch for him and an orange juice and tonic water for myself.

'I don't know how you can drink that stuff, old boy,' he said, as I drained my glass. 'I did a piece on cyclamates in soft drinks once. I've never touched one since.' He scooped another handful of peanuts into his mouth and dropped the empty bag onto the floor. 'I'll tell you something I did come across when I was doing my article on them. Ruth Armstrong isn't so pure as she would like you to believe.'

'Yeah?'

'She had an illegitimate kid when she was young. Maybe that's why she's so against sex now. Same way ex-alcoholics turn against drink in such a fanatical way. You're not an ex-alkie, old boy, are you?'

'No. I'm just easing up for a while.'

'Good idea,' he approved. 'Keep meaning to do it myself.' He took a swallow of his fresh drink. 'There was nothing I could go into print with about Ruth Armstrong's illegitimate kid. But there was enough there to convince me.'

Further along the bar a man was attempting to balance a cheese biscuit on the end of a dog's nose. The biscuit fell to the floor, and the dog immediately ate it.

'What's the set-up with the Friends of the Inner Light?' I asked.

'The usual old mish-mash of alternative religion, holistic healing, pop-psychology and general bollocks,' he said. 'You have to be really dedicated to join the Inner Circle itself. That's when you become one of the Guides and spread the word. But they give courses and classes that anyone can go to. As long as the anyone has enough money to pay.'

'You don't have to be celibate for that.'

'They advise it, but don't insist on it.'

Behind him the man who had been attempting to teach the dog tricks crouched to balance a biscuit on his own nose by way of demonstration. As the biscuit fell to the floor, the dog gobbled it up.

'Have you met Pete the handyman?' I asked.

'Oh yes. He comes here sometimes. Bit of a dodgy customer, if you ask me.'

'Did you investigate him, too?'

'No. He wasn't working for them when I did my article. But I wouldn't be surprised if he's done time. He has that look about him. Reformed junkie from what I hear. Though I don't know so much about the reformed part. Again, nothing I'd go into print with. But –'

'Vibes.'

'Exactly. I wouldn't be surprised if his girlfriend isn't on something, too. Though she isn't bad to look at. If you don't mind them without tits.'

'What does she look like?'

He described Toorey Dunphee, near enough, and then pushed his empty glass towards me.

'Just a single this time, old boy,' he said. 'I shouldn't drink so much mid-week. I'm trying to cut down.'

'She sounds alright,' I said, as I signalled the barman again.

'Yeah. Funny sort of face. But it grows on you after a while. She's looked a bit rough some of the times she's been in here with him, though. When they haven't been able to score, probably. I'm sure I saw needle marks on her thigh one night when I was having a butcher's up her skirt. They can go on using it for years, some of them, you know. If they can manage to keep it under control.' He frowned. 'Oh alright, then,' he said, as if finally giving into my constant urging. 'Make it a large one. I'll follow your example and have a complete break from it tomorrow night.'

Thirteen

The man who ran the folk club in the top room of the Happy Mason turned out to be a tall, amiable fellow in his fifties, wearing one of the sky-blue 'Fisherman's smocks' I had seen advertised in the back pages of the *Observer*. I had almost sent off for one, but some instinct had stopped me from writing out the cheque. Now that I saw the smock on the man, I realised my instinct had been correct. It made him look like a Farnham antique dealer.

The folk club was something of a hobby for him. By day he worked in some government office. He did tell me what he did, but I forgot even as he was telling me. It was my guess that if he hadn't decided to run a folk club, it would have been a film society instead. He was that sort of man. Why Torrey had walked out without finishing her set, he had no idea. She had played previous dates, and there had been no trouble. The man thought Toorey had a lot of talent. He thought she could do well on television. He didn't seem as pissed off about the incident as Brian Paxton had made out. Just a little sad, if anything. I left him frowning over a crackling speaker that was giving trouble and made my way over to the bar in the corner.

My order of tonic water and orange juice caused some amusement among the hirsute types clustered around, guzzling 'Clogmaster's Brew' or 'Gurney's Passing Strange Ale'. One of them even went so far as to affect theatrical horror, throwing one hand to his brow as he stared at the arc of skewered lemon floating around the top of my glass.

Restraining an urge to kick him in the goolies, I carried my drink over to an empty chair near a small raised platform. There was a woman on the platform, occupying most of its space. She had long, dark hair, mournful eyes, and a dress that could have been styled by 'Black's of Greenock'. There was a guitar slung around her neck, hanging from a brightly embroidered strap.

In her mouth was a small pitch pipe with which she was attempting to tune the steel strings of her guitar. Conscious of the waning attention of her audience, she occasionally removed the pitch-pipe to deliver a humorous aside. The humorous asides were done in a Goon voice – the Esperanto of the folk world. But when at last she began to sing, it was no laughing matter.

The lyrics of her first song centred around a disaster that had taken place some hundred years ago in a Cornish tin mine. There were no survivors. Nor was there a great deal of applause. Unfazed by the lack of response, the woman put the pitch pipe back in her mouth and tinkered around until she found an approximation of an open G tuning. With this accomplished, she gave us 'The Ballad of Jake Magee', a seemingly interminable story of a life filled with misfortune and hardship, leading at last to the gallows. We were invited to sing along with the chorus of this one, but few of us took her up on the invitation.

Following a light powdering of polite applause, the woman moved onto a song that she claimed would be in 17th century Portuguese – a claim none of us felt bold enough to dispute. Graciously, the woman provided a precis in English. It was a grim tale of murder, rape, betrayal, revenge, and, of course, tragedy. Once more, there were no survivors. The musical accompaniment was suitably stark – just a banging of the dampened strings with the hand. The woman's nails were chewed down to the quick, I noticed. It was a long, long haul and as her voice trailed off into a quivering moan, the audience lapsed into a cataleptic silence.

'Blind Billee' was the tale of a cabin boy, blinded at the Battle of Trafalgar and subsequently subjected to sixty years of bitter bad luck. There was a verse for each of his sixty doom-laden years. Each and every verse was followed by a chorus.

When the woman came to the end of her set, intermittent attempts at conversation were made by those around me still capable of speech. I tried to make it to my feet. But my legs had gone. I couldn't get up. I recalled reading an article in some magazine about 'psychic vampires'. These people possess strong negative vibes and can drain your energy by simply being around you, leaving you limp and exhausted. From the way I was feeling now, the woman was a psychic Bride of Dracula.

A rustle of movement caught my attention as a sprightly old gent stepped up to the mike. He was several sizes too small for the Fair Isle pullover and baggy grey trousers he wore. His face was scrubbed bright pink, and before commencing to sing he discreetly removed his top dentures and slipped them in his pocket. He sang with one gnarled old hand cupped around an ear and his voice was high and pure. The songs centred around life on a Suffolk farm at the turn of the century and were performed in a thick, near-incomprehensible dialect. He took Muswell Hill by storm and had the hirsute yakahoos standing around the bar shouting for encore after encore.

Again I attempted to rise to my feet. But my legs felt as if they were trapped in quick-drying cement. A heavy depression began to enclose me. It was a depression that Kevin and Sylvie did nothing to alleviate.

An earthy, unrelentingly jolly young couple, Kevin and Sylvie drew upon a vast repertoire devoted to randy chivalry – randy knights, chastity belts and much play upon words like 'weapon' or 'lance'. An instant hit, they had the yakahoos at the bar fa la la-la-ing from the start. I found myself beginning to develop a slight, but evident headache. Evident enough for me to wish the yakahoos would stop banging their pewter tankards of foaming ale on the bar counter.

I was willing myself to my feet when a young kid with a twelve string guitar came on. He looked as wholesome and as dumb as a member of the Walton family, but he had a great voice – a resonant low tenor with just enough edge to stop it from being too sweet. He began his set with a song he had written himself. A slowish, sad number about loneliness and lost love. Rain featured heavily. Leaves fell, doors closed and telephones rang unanswered. I enjoyed it. My headache eased up a little.

The young guy played a nice finger-picking accompaniment in a style I had been attempting to master for years, without success. Like the downbeat Earth Mother we had listened to earlier, he too used open tunings. But he used them well, producing the full ringing sound they were intended to have. He followed the sad song with a gently rocking moving-on-down-the-line type number, getting in a few riffs that had me shaking my head in admiration and envy. Then he announced that he was going to sing a song written by Toorey Dunphee.

It was just another love song. It didn't say anything that hadn't been said before by other, and better, songs. But like Toorey's funny, pointy face, it grew on you. I began to feel a tremendous sense of loss for something I couldn't quite define. I grieved for a lover I had never known. For a youth I had never experienced. For places I had never seen.

If I had been a drinking man, I would probably have broken down and wept.

I had perked up a bit by the time he sang his last number, a rag-time blues. When he had finished, I went over to him at the bar.

'You play a mean guitar,' I told him.

He shrugged in a self-deprecating manner.

'I keep practising,' he said. 'But it still sounds shit to me.'

There was a CND badge fixed to his faded blue denim jacket. Underneath it was a Robinson's marmalade golly. When I assured him again that his playing was terrific, he smiled and nodded like a toy dog in the rear window of a Ford Consul. The nod and the smile took me back to California and a girl I had known in San Francisco. I was trying to remember just why we had broken up when I felt a presence at my side.

I turned to face a stunning golden-haired beauty, with a fresh, clear complexion and pale amber eyes that did things to the pit of my stomach. If I had been a hundred years younger, I would have fallen instantly and hopelessly in love with her. The girl didn't even see me. She was conscious only of the big, amiable, dumb-looking youth standing in front of me. For his part, he didn't seem to find her that special. But isn't that always the way?

'You said you'd call round for me,' the girl accused.

The young guy shrugged indifferently.

'I didn't have time,' he said. 'I had some things to do first. Sorry.'

'It doesn't matter,' she said, in a way that implied it mattered very much.

As they both stood there, not saying anything, I dragged myself back to the reason I had come there in the first place.

'That was a nice song,' I complimented. 'That one by Toorey Dunphee.'

He switched on the nodding smile again, making me slightly dizzy.

'It is a nice song, isn't it? One of my favourites. Toorey writes good material. Do you know Toorey?'

'Friend of a friend.'

'She's a nice lady,' he said.

There was a derisive sound from my side.

'If you're into that generation,' said the dazzling beauty.

Her large sensual lips turned into a sneer quite turned me on. I wondered what she would look like in long, black leather boots.

Conscious of my attention, her amber eyes roamed my features but seemed to find nothing of interest, save for a momentary pausing on the loose skin hanging under my jowls and the hair growing out of my nostrils.

'Were you here the night Toorey walked out before finishing her set?' I asked, turning away, deeply depressed again.

'Yes. I was actually. Very weird. I don't know why she did it. Though she had been edgy that night. Even her singing was off. Off for her that is. For anyone else, it would have been fantastic. Toorey's got a great voice. Easy and natural. Relaxed.'

'Like a female Val Doonican on heroin,' chipped in the heartbreaking beauty standing next to me. 'My mum and dad would probably like her. If they didn't know she was a junkie.'

'Shut up, Fizz,' he snapped angrily, losing his cool.

'It's true.'

'I don't care. Just shut up.'

'It's okay,' I said. 'I knew about Toorey using heroin.'

'She's not really a junkie, you know,' he said, wanting to believe it, I thought. 'She has it under control.'

'Don't they all,' said La Belle Dame Sans Merci.

A couple of bearded hearties pushed through to call for pints of 'Entwhistle's Harvester's Handicap', or some such. I turned back to the boy.

'I don't suppose you've any idea where Toorey went?' I asked.

'I was going to ask you the same question.'

'What about Pete? Do you know her boyfriend Pete?'

'Hah,' the young goddess by my side sneered again.

I found myself filled with near uncontrollable lust. I told myself that the end of desire was the end of unhappiness. But the message failed to get below my waist. I wanted a long and very dirty weekend with Fizz. But I knew the chances were nil. She belonged to the boy body and soul, his to do as he pleased. And from what I could sense, he was hung up on Toorey. I wished I had tried harder to master a finger-picking style.

'Pete?' Fizz mocked. 'Another of her young swains. Younger men just love her. If they had awards for cradle snatching, they'd give Toorey an Oedipus.'

'Fizz. Just shut up, will you?'

'Oh, sorry, Tim,' she apologised with heavy sarcasm. 'I'd quite forgotten you were another of Toorey's little puppies.'

'I am not one of her little puppies. I happen to like her. Very much. And she likes me. We have a lot in common. She makes nice music and she sings nice songs.'

'Is she a good fuck?' Fizz asked, in a tense, provocative manner.

The boy made a show of thinking.

'Yes,' he said at last. 'As a matter of fact, she is. A lot better than you. A whole lot better.'

Fizz reacted as if he had suddenly slapped her around the face. She reddened, and tears filled her eyes. She started to say something, stopped, then turned and hurried away to the exit. We watched her go. She had a terrific arse, I thought.

'Women,' the young guy said, showing me his Californian smile again.

He didn't seem bothered by her departure. He probably knew she would be back.

I wondered about ordering a triple vodka, but settled for another tonic water and orange. My young friend with the magical power over beautiful women had a cider. As I waited to be served, the Earth Mother lumbered back onto the platform, starting a rush for the bar. Throwing her head back in a

dramatic gesture, she sang of 'Poor Ned Tyler'. Ned's parents were crushed to death under the hooves of the king's horses during a food riot, setting the poor young orphan onto a life of crime.

'Funnily enough, I didn't really go to bed with Toorey,' the boy said, as I handed him his cider. 'I wanted to. How I wanted to. I don't know why quite. It isn't that she's beautiful or anything.'

'But there's something about her.'

'Right.' He sighed. 'But she just didn't seem interested in me that way. I just didn't do anything for her physically. I could tell by the way she looked at me. Do you know what I mean?'

'Yeah. Your girl friend just gave me the same look.'

But he didn't hear me.

'Toorey treated me like a younger brother, I suppose,' he said, wistfully. 'I kept hoping it would turn into something else. But it never did. Though I still can't understand why she was going around with Pete.

'Who knows why anybody goes around with anybody,' I said, sinking into a deeper gloom.

Things weren't going well for Poor Ned Tyler either. The Earth Mother was only thirty or forty verses in, but the poor sod had already lost his arm to a ball fired from a dragoon's musket, contracted syphilis, and was currently doing a spell in Newgate nick.

'I wouldn't be surprised if Pete isn't some sort of criminal,' the young guy said, frowning like a child trying to look like an adult. 'Maybe he has control of her through her habit. Not that it really is a habit.'

'It never is.'

'Toorey's different,' he said, taking offence at my tone. 'She's got it under control. She just takes it to help with her work. She's a very creative person. A lot of creative people take drugs.'

'Maybe,' I agreed, suddenly tired. 'Listen, do you have Toorey's address?'

He looked at me with sudden suspicion.

'I thought you were a friend of hers,' he said.

'I am. But I've lost my address book.'

'Are you the police?' he asked, in a hostile way.

'The police don't wear white shoes.'

'I don't give a shit if you are. You can fuck off. I'm not telling you where she lives. You've just been pumping me. Trying to find out about her. I thought you were a fellow musician. And all you are is a pig.'

'I'm not,' I protested. 'Honest.'

'Just fuck off.'

He stood glowering at me until I turned to leave. Just as I got to the door, the Earth Mother announced to the rows of empty seats that she was about to sing 'Jim Lassiter's in his Cold Clay Grave'.

Fourteen

I went down the stairs and started making my way across the crowded saloon bar, recognizing many fellow refugees from the Earth Mother. Halfway across the room, I altered direction and headed for the Gents'. The signs led me along a small, damp-smelling corridor out into a yard. From there I followed my nose.

The urinal was clogged with dog-ends and the smell was terrible, making me grateful for the broken window above my head. I could still hear the Earth Mother in the distance – not enough to hear how things were going for Jim Lassiter, but I could make a good guess. As I relieved myself of the build-up of tonic water and orange juice, I read the graffiti scrawled on the wall facing me. Someone called Ken offered to bugger me with his fourteen-inch cock, but only if I was a young boy between fourteen and seventeen, and preferably blond. Roger, by contrast, offered to take on all comers but omitted to give his measurements. There was a lot of racial stuff – democratically including the blacks, the Pakistanis, the Jews, the Irish, the Japanese, the Germans, the Spanish, the Argentinians, and even the Icelanders.

I was zipping up my flies and just finishing off a highly improbable story about the writer's childhood experience with a nymphomaniac auntie, when three young guys came in.

For some reason I sensed trouble and by the way they were blocking the exit I was sure I was right.

'You've been putting your nose in where it isn't wanted,' said the one nearest to me.

'Oh yes?' I said, sizing them up.

None of them was big enough to count as a heavy, but they looked nasty enough to be trouble. I was going to have to stay on my feet. If they got me on the floor, their Doc Martins were going to give me a bad stomping.

'Yes you have.'

'Are you friends of Pete's?'

'We're nobody's friends, mate,' said the one blocking the door. 'You're going to get a right going-over.'

'Oh yes?' I said again, stalling for time.

'Casualty ward job,' the nearest of them assured me.

Above us, the Earth Mother stopped singing. There was no applause. I became aware of the hissing of a leaky cistern in one of the lavatories.

'I don't suppose there's any way I can talk you out of this?' I asked.

'No chance.'

'Oh well,' I said, with a resigned shrug.

I stepped back and kicked him in the balls. My heel was on target and connected with a satisfactory impact, but my other heel skidded on the slippery, garbage-strewn floor. I lost my balance and did the one thing I had told myself not to do. I fell onto the floor.

As the Doc Martin boots came in, I rolled into a drunkard's stance – a fighting position adopted while lying on the ground. I deflected the worst of the kicks while I looked for an opening to catch one of them off balance.

The one I had kicked in the balls was being sick into the far corner. But his friends were plenty for me to handle. More than I could handle, I thought, as one of the boots caught me painfully in the thigh.

I shoved my heel out hard and managed to connect with a shin.

'Bastard,' a voice above me said, in pain.

I rolled away from a boot directed at my head. It missed, but caught my shoulder.

'Bastard,' I groaned.

I shifted, and turned, blocked and kicked. But I was tiring. It looked like the casualty ward could expect my custom.

I was about to make one final effort and attempt to pull them both down onto the ground with me, when the door burst open to a human whirlwind.

It was over within seconds. Neither of them had a chance. One of them managed to make a run for it, but his friend was laid out cold, next to the one who was still retching into the corner.

My rescuer looked down at me and shook his head despairingly.

'Call yourself a student of the martial arts? You're bloody hopeless.'

'Ah, but I'm not a black belt, Mr Skindle. Unlike your good self. Also, I lack the natural vicious streak you possess.'

I climbed to my feet. There was a lot of pain scattered around my body, and my legs felt shaky. But I wasn't going to strain the resources of the National Health.

Skindle turned to look at the fallen.

'They're even more hopeless than you,' he jeered. 'You don't get the class of villains you used to.'

'Except for one or two notable exceptions like yourself, Mr Skindle.'

Skindle turned back to me. He was a short, thick-set man, wearing a blue track-suit and orange and green training shoes. He was bald unless you counted the pale fuzz that covered his scalp.

'I hear you've been taking my name in vain,' he said. 'That is a very serious offence. We can't have the likes of you going around impersonating officers of the law.'

'Ex-officers of the law,' I pointed out.

'Don't get funny with me, son,' he warned, giving my nose a painful, playful tap with one of his short, blunt fingers. 'I don't take kindly to attempts at taking the piss out of me.'

'I'll remember that,' I said, suddenly blinded by the tears that the tap had loosened.

Skindle returned to his mock-jocular manner.

'Some of my former colleagues had occasion to visit certain premises in the Bayswater area, concerning the matter of a stolen motorcycle and side-car.'

'Stolen?' I said, surprised.

'Yes. A highly criminal offence. But that, as it turned out, was merely the tip of the iceberg. When apprehended in their premises, the suspects were found to be in the possession of illegal substances.'

'You don't mean drugs?' I said.

'Half a pound of Afghan Red and four ounces of Charley.'

'Afghan Red?' I sneered derisively. 'Come off it. There hasn't ɔeen any of that around in about four years.'

We moved aside as a couple of men came in to use the urinal. They glanced at the guy retching in the corner and the one laid ɔut beside him.

'Glue sniffers,' Skindle explained. 'Hard to see what pleasure :hey get out of it, isn't it?'

The explanation seemed to satisfy them and they carried on ρerforming the function they had come in for.

'Four ounces of Charley?' I questioned Skindle when they nad gone.

Skindle shrugged apologetically.

'Well, you know how the lads are sometimes. A bit keen to make a good impression. They want to make it look good on the arrest sheet, so they bring along some of the stuff they've impounded. As it turned out, I believe they genuinely did find something. About a quarter of Paki Black.'

'Just enough for a few smokes.'

'It's still illegal. They'd committed a criminal offence. So there's no harm in boosting it a bit. After all, there's no innocent party involved.'

'Very reassuring.'

'But here's the good bit. You're never going to guess what those two little berks told the arresting officers. They said a policeman had given them that quarter of Paki Black.'

'Go on. I find that hard to credit.'

'It gets better. They said this copper sat around rolling joints for them. Something to do with a public relations exercise, he told them.'

'It sounds like they were tripping on drugs.'

'Do you know what they said this copper's name was? The one who was sitting there rolling those joints for them? Detective Sergeant Skindle of West End Central.'

'Never. I find that hard to believe of a man with your impeccable record. I hope they hang for perjury.'

Skindle flicked the end of my nose again, producing a fresh flow of tears.

'What were this lot going to do you over for? You been

messing about with someone's else's tart?'

'No. I think they were just trying to mug me,' I said, making a snap decision to tell him as little about my activities as possible.

'Stupid sods. Come on, son,' he said, resting one of his hands on my shoulder and pressing gently into a nerve centre.

'Where are we going?' I asked anxiously.

'You're going to drive me home. My car's packed up. Do you know how to get to Pinner from here?'

Fifteen

During our drive I asked Skindle how he had known I would be at the Happy Mason, but he insisted on remaining smugly enigmatic as he rattled on about 'routine police procedures'. Annoying as he was, I felt more concern about who had sicked the down-market muscle onto me. Eliminating my employer Captain Midnight from my list of suspects, I was left with Brian Paxton or his secretary Linda.

Skindle coughed and lit another cigarette. I rolled the window down further. I switched on the radio and twiddled around until I found some Schumann piano pieces. Skindle formed a counterpoint by whistling a selection of the latest Top Ten hits.

We drove deeper into suburbia until my guide directed me to stop outside one in a row of identical Thirties houses with pebble dash walls and Crittall windows. The wooden gate leading to Skindle's residence was fretworked with a rising sun design. Looking through the fretwork sun I could see a gravel path leading up to the house.

'Come on, son,' Skindle said, as I sat, making no attempt to leave the car. 'I'll give you a nice cup of cocoa. Don't make too much noise when we get in. The missus will have gone up to bed.'

I climbed out of the car, locked it and followed Skindle up the gravel path. Gnomes roamed free across a neatly clipped lawn bordered by an equally neat privet hedge. Most of the flowers were dead or dying by now, but the flower beds were tidily kept, with no trace of weeds or fallen leaves. On a wall above the front window was a bird box disguised as a miniature Swiss chalet. Lit by the strange yellow of the street-lighting, the whole place took on the air of a German expressionist film.

Skindle put a key in the lock, opened the door and motioned for me to follow. I stepped inside as he switched on a light and held a finger up to his lips, reminding me to be quiet. My face stared back at me from a small mirror fixed to a combined barometer and clothes-brush hanger. Next to it was a wooden plaque holding a tiny pair of Dutch clogs. Dolls of all nations lined the shelves of a small alcove opposite. My nostrils were assailed by the mixed odours of lemon furniture polish, lavender floor wax and pine window cleaner.

We continued along the hallway, passing portraits of weeping clowns and tinted photographs of small furry animals playing with wool or wearing comical hats. We stopped outside a door where Skindle reminded me once again of the need to be silent. Glancing furtively towards the short wooden staircase that led presumably to the bedroom where his wife lay sleeping, he opened the door.

I stepped into a small kitchen where the smells changed to those of Domestos, washing powder and roasting meat.

'Should be alright now,' Skindle said, picking up an oven glove and putting it on. 'The old cow's deaf in one ear. It's just that she stays awake listening for me sometimes. I'll give you a word of advice, old mate. Don't ever get married. Not even if you think you'll never get another bunk-up in your whole life. It still isn't worth it.'

He walked over to the oven, opened the door and took out a plate of food. A chop, roast potatoes and peas. It looked good. I began to feel hungry.

'Dried up to buggery,' Skindle complained, somewhat churlishly I felt. 'Stupid bitch left the oven too high. Don't ever get married. And don't take a job where you can get forced into early retirement. It's a bloody living death. When I was working, I hardly noticed the old cow was here.'

'You can't spare a bit, can you?' I asked, as he set the plate down on a table and took a knife and fork out of a drawer.

Skindle sat down.

'You can have anything I leave. Alright?'

I had a brief but vivid memory of his eating habits.

'No. I've suddenly lost my appetite. What did you want to see me about? I suppose that's what you want. Unless you just happened to be passing the Happy Mason by chance.'

Skindle tore out a section of meat with his knife and fork,

performing like a mad surgeon in a nightmare. He stuck the section of charred flesh in his mouth and chewed.

'Burnt to buggery,' he pronounced. 'Right. There are two things I want to see you about, my son. First, and not least, we might be able to do a little business together again. Highly financially rewarding business.'

'Oh yes,' I said without enthusiasm. I had once been blackmailed by Skindle into doing some dubious business with him. Although, I had to admit, I had made a reasonable amount of money from the affair.

'I can see you're overjoyed,' Skindle cackled, pointing a forkful of food at me, while he let gravy dribble down his chin. 'I knew you'd be pleased.'

'What's the second thing?' I asked, feeling I might never be hungry again.

'I want your advice on a couple of my paintings. Funny, I seem to have improved since you got the boot from the school.'

Before the art school where I taught had made me redundant, Skindle had been one of my pupils. It was a fee-paying establishment. None of its students would have earned a place in any decent art school, where ability would have been a condition of entry. Least of all Skindle. I found him in my Life Drawing class, where his work was distinguished only by its creator's curious obsession with pubic hair, drawing each individual hair with a hard, black pencil.

'Don't tell me you've got a show in Bond Street. On second thoughts, don't tell me. I'd rather not know. Tell me about this financially rewarding business.'

'Ah, you are interested,' he said, pointing another forkful of food at me.

'Would it make any difference if I said no?'

'None at all, old mate. Bung the kettle on, will you?'

He emptied most of a salt shaker over his plate, added a pool of HP sauce, and then began stirring the mixture around with his fork.

'You said cocoa,' I complained. 'I've been brought here under false pretences. I shall have to ring my solicitor.'

'We'll have the cocoa later,' he said, reassuringly. 'Plenty of time. I like a cup of tea after my grub. Nothing like it.'

I found an electric kettle, filled it from a polished tap over a spotless sink, then plugged it into a point over a sideboard.

There was a wooden plaque cut from a tree trunk at my eyelevel. The plaque bore a homily, burnt into its surface with the end of a hot poker.

> Dear Friend
> Within this house you'll want for naught
> Not bread, nor wine, nor brew
> We only ask if taken short
> You'll kindly use the loo.'

'Very profound,' I said. 'The Bhagavad Gita, isn't it?'

'The missus. She did it at evening class. The artistic streak seems to run in the family.' He stopped, poked around the inside of his mouth with a forefinger, then pulled out a morsel of chewed meat. 'Do you think that looks a bit off?' he asked.

'I couldn't say. Not without throwing up. No wonder the pigs are called pigs. They even eat like them.'

Skindle became stern.

'Mind your lip, lad. I enjoy a joke as much as the next man. But don't overstep the mark. Otherwise you'll wish you hadn't.'

I pulled a chair out from under the table and sat down. In another part of the house I could hear a cuckoo clock sounding eleven.

Skindle ate, if that was the word, in silence for a few moments. Then he said, 'Your mate Captain Midnight has been pulling your pisser, old son.

'I rather thought he might have been.'

'Oh yes, he has.' Skindle exploded a mouthful of food as he laughed. 'I'm surprised at you, Stanley.'

'Nobody calls me Stanley.'

'I just did. I called you Stanley because you're a right wally.'

'I am.'

As the cuckoo clock finished, the announcement of the hour was taken up by some muffled chimes.

'I didn't know you were quite so sentimental. All that stuff about broken hearts and dying of love. You'll have to have a browse through my old woman's collection of Mills and Boon. Just your sort of thing.'

He exploded with laughter again. I wiped food from my raincoat.

'So what are you now, then?' he asked. 'Some kind of private detective? Not your style at all, old son. Not at all. You haven't got a logical mind. You couldn't deduce your way out of a paper bag.'

'I work on intuition a lot. I use the right-hand side of my brain more than my left.'

'Your brains are in your bollocks most of the time. I wouldn't hire you to find a missing elephant in a council flat.'

'I haven't set up as a private eye,' I told him. 'I was just doing a sort of favour for a sort of friend.'

'You were doing a sort of favour for five hundred quid.'

'How do you know so much about it?'

Skindle dropped the knife and fork onto the plate and pushed it over to me.

'Do you want this?' he asked. 'I think the meat's off.'

'No thanks.'

Skindle lit a cigarette.

'I had a little talk with your mate Captain Midnight. During the pursuit of certain aspects of a business affair I am conducting, it became necessary for me to have a word with him.'

'This is the same business matter you wish to involve me in, I take it?'

Skindle feigned astonishment.

'Very good. That must be the right-hand part of your brain working. Now I'll tell you why Captain Midnight really wants you to find Toorey Dunphee. Are you sitting comfortably?'

'No. These chairs are very badly designed.'

'Blame the missus. She thought they went with the curtains or some bollocks.' He broke off for a cough and a quick drag on his cigarette before continuing. 'The real reason he wants you to find Toorey and her boyfriend Pete is they burned him on a deal. He set them up with a buyer for a kilo of coke. And they skipped off without paying him his five per cent.'

'Nasty.'

'It gets worse, old son. They did a naughty with the buyer, too. They let him taste a sample and then worked a switch with a bag of talcum powder. He was right pissed off.'

'I'll bet. A kilo of cocaine. That's got to be worth around seventy thousand quid at current prices. Things could get heavy with that kind of money involved.'

'They could do. But they won't.'

'No?'

The kettle began to boil. I got up, found a couple of mugs and a box of teabags on the sideboard. I put a bag in each of the mugs.

'No,' Skindle scoffed, as I poured hot water into the mugs. 'This is Act of God stuff. No comeback. One of Fate's backhanders to the pure in heart. The coke belonged to a couple of amateurs. Hooray Henrys trying to make a quick couple of bob to cover the rising cost of caviar. They got panicky when they saw a customs launch in their binoculars. Dumped all their goodies overboard. It got washed up on the beach at Weston-super-Mare a few days later. A bloke walking his dog found it. Being a man of outstanding moral character, he reported his find to the local police.'

'Who instantly went into business for themselves,' I suggested, poking the teabags around with a spoon.

'Now, now,' he cautioned, becoming momentarily stern again. 'As it happened, somebody was able to go into business for himself. One of the local young undesirables happens to come along before the bloke walking his dog. Don't ask me what he was doing up at that hour. He finds one of the bags of Charley. Tumbles what it is. And pisses off with it. Fast. He's in clover. A kilo of coke. The owners are in custody. And they're only a couple of Hooray Henrys anyway. And nobody knows the bag he's got is missing. The little bugger's laughing.'

I handed Skindle one of the mugs, then went across to the fridge to find a bottle of milk.

'I have a feeling he didn't keep on laughing,' I said, as I brought the bottle back to the table.

'You're a pessimist, old son. That's your trouble. You spend too much time dabbling in alternative religions. All that Eastern stuff about reincarnation and coming back for another go and ending up married to someone like my missus again. That's enough to depresss the bollocks off anyone.' He sipped his tea and made a face. 'Where's the bloody sugar then? I can't drink tea without sugar. In the cupboard. Second shelf.'

I went over to the cupboard and found a small plastic bowl containing sugar cubes.

'Why shouldn't everything work out for him?' Skindle continued, taking four of the sugar cubes and dropping them into his mug. 'No one knows the stuff is missing. He hasn't got the law after him. There are no villains toasting his grey-haired old mum's feet with a soldering iron.'

'I still have this feeling that things ended up going wrong for him.'

'As it happens, you're right. Must be your woman's intuition again.'

I began to feel sore from where the Doc Martin boots had connected, and my headache was starting up again. I was tempted to ask Skindle for aspirins, but I didn't want him jeering at me for being a cissy who couldn't take a beating-up every now and then.

'I don't suppose you've got any aspirin or paracetamol?' I said, giving in as the headache got worse.

'Oh,' Skindle jeered. 'Have you got a headache from playing with those nasty, rough boys? You'll live. Now, this little nerk who's got the stuff doesn't know how to unload it. He hasn't got any contacts in Weston-super-Mare. Not any who can handle anything like a kilo of coke. So he gives this mate of his a ring – a real Jack the Lad who did time with him when they were both trainee petty criminals. Can you guess who this mate is?'

'Pete?'

'Very good indeed. I'm going to have to look into this right-hand brain stuff. Pete it is. And he says he can handle it easy. Always had a lot of mouth. Very cocky. Bung it up to him on the Red Star express, he says. Safe as houses. Better than the post. And quicker. All he's got to do is let Pete know the time of the train it's arriving on and bingo. I don't know what percent Pete said he'd charge him for unloading it. But it was a load of old bollocks anyway. He wasn't going to give the poor, trusting little sod anything. Still, the trusting little sod wasn't to know that. So he does like he is told and bungs it on the Red Star.'

'What went wrong?' I asked.

I wondered if one of my ribs was cracked, or merely bruised. The pain was getting worse all over now.

'Nothing this end. Pete picked up the parcel alright.'

'What happened at the other end?'

'The little nerk ran into the back of a stationary lorry on his way home from sending off the parcel. Pissed probably. Or out of his bonce on something or other. Does himself all sorts of nasty. He's lying there leaking vital bodily fluids and bits of bone and gristle over the public highway, when a police officer arrives upon the scene.'

'Aha,' I said. 'I think his troubles are about to start.'

Skindle looked indignant as he ground his cigarette out in a novelty ashtray, fashioned in the shape of a dolphin holding a plate on its head.

'The police officer instantly calls for an ambulance and gets him to hospital. His prompt action probably saved the little nerk's life.'

'Who lived to regret it.'

'Right again, my son. A couple of days later. When the little nerk is off the critical list and feeling well enough to have a peek down the nurse's uniform when she tucks him in, the police officer calls to see him. To take down a statement about his accident. Using the right-hand side of his brain,' Skindle paused to give a deferential nod in my direction, 'the police officer gets a feeling that the victim had been flying on some chemical or other. Long hair. "Coal Not Dole" sticker, CND badge. Scruffy appearance. Need I say more?'

'I don't think prejudice is located in the right-hand side of the brain.'

'Never mind. Now. When the police officer mentions drugs, the little nerk becomes very worried. The officer becomes suspicious. Sensing villainy, he pursues his enquiries with a little more vigour – threatening various methods of breaking the little nerk's body so that he spends the rest of his life in hospital. The nerk instantly breaks down and tells him all about the coke.'

'A heartening triumph for the forces of law and order.

They've made the streets of Weston-super-Mare safe for women and children to walk in once again.'

'Now. Here's where it gets really interesting,' Skindle said, ignoring me. 'This police officer happens to be a mate of mine.'

'Aha. That's enough to have the poor little nerk screaming for a bedpan.'

'We were in the same division together,' Skindle said, leaning back in his chair, lighting another cigarette. 'At least we were until some rather nasty allegations of corruption forced him to be transferred to Weston-super-Mare. Nothing was proved of course. But he was transferred all the same.'

'These allegations were totally unfounded, I take it?'

'Not at all, old mate. They were absolutely true. Every one of them. We were running a very nice little protection racket among the local prossies until one of them shopped us. But he was a good bloke, and he kept me out of it. We stayed in touch. Doing a little business together every now and then. When he stumbled over this lot, he thought there might be something in it for us.'

I got up and walked stiffly and painfully over to the sideboard to plug in the electric kettle. I went back for my mug and carried it over to the sink. Skindle watched me with an amused expression on his face.

'Hot mustard bath,' he recommended. 'Make you feel as good as new. I don't think much of your kung fu, the shape you're in.'

'I haven't been practising as much as I should. I'm going to start going to classes more often.'

'So,' Skindle said, taking up his narrative once more. 'I take myself off to Paddington Station to have a chat with the bloke in the Red Star parcel section. Very conscientious bloke running the place. Very strong on identification of people who've picked up parcels. I gave him a quick shufti of my old identification card and told him I was making enquiries about a villain who had picked up a parcel from him. I was able to give him the time of the train, of course. Thanks to my mate in Weston-super-Mare.'

Skindle paused to pull at a small strip of cigarette paper that had stuck to his bottom lip.

'Now, as it happens, this bloke in the parcels department remembered the chap who had picked this one up. He had found him suspicious –'

'Long hair. "Coal Not Dole" sticker. CND badge. Scruffy appearance.'

'That sort of thing. Yes. He'd made this bloke produce his driving licence and a couple of letters with his name and address on them. He copied the address down in his book. Peter Barnes, 32 Gilmour Street, Kentish Town. I went along there. Bunch of religious nutters. Pete was their handyman or something. They gave him a room rent free in return for doing odd jobs about the place. They knew he was a villain. Maybe they were hoping to convert him or something. Pointless. You can't change the criminal mentality. Anyway Pete had scarpered. Done a sudden bunk.'

The kettle began to boil. I got up slowly and went over to make my tea. I wondered if the tin decorated with a reproduction of Millais's 'Bubbles' contained biscuits. I looked inside and found some chocolate digestives.

'Alright if I have one of these?' I asked.

'Help yourself. They've been there about a year.'

I took out a biscuit, broke it in half and put one of the sections in my mouth. It was soggy and tasted vaguely of paraffin. All the same I continued eating it.

'Well, I ask around locally in the shops and that. But none of them know where he is. But I do find out about his girl friend Toorey. I also find out about another bloke who's been around asking about him. The description fits someone I used to know in a professional capacity. Captain Midnight.'

'Professional capacity? He's a nark, is he?'

'He sells the law a bit of information, now and then. He'd sell out his own mother if he knew who she was. I still use him now and then. When the need arises. He's a hard lad to get hold of if he doesn't want to be found. But I caught up with him in the end. I found out where he was having his car serviced.'

'Betrayed by the love of a car. You've seen the movie, now read the manual.'

Skindle laughed. Fortunately I was far enough away not to be covered in spittle and worse.

'I almost pissed myself when he told me about hiring you. Of course he wasn't going to tell me anything at all, at first. Not until I hit him in the gut. Then he was very co-operative. It all worked out very nicely in the end. To everybody's satisfaction.'

'Oh yes?' I asked doubtfully, chewing on another soggy chocolate biscuit.

'Very amicable arrangement. You carry on with what you're doing. Looking for Pete and Toorey. Only now you report back to me. There'll be a few bob in it for you. I'll double up on what Captain Midnight was going to pay you. A grand.'

'Why don't you go ahead and find them yourself? You're better at that sort of thing than I am.'

'I'd stand out too much in the circles you'll be moving in. I look like a copper. But you'll blend in nicely. You could be anything from a raging poofter to a mad poet looking for a fix. Anyway, I want to keep a low profile. Just in case anything goes wrong. It wouldn't do for an ex-officer of the law to be seen to be involved in this kind of thing. I'm prepared to help, of course. I have access to information that might not otherwise be obtainable. Should you need them, consider police records at your disposal.'

'That's very kind of you. Supposing I don't want to play?'

Skindle smiled as he shook his head dismissively.

'Don't even consider it, old son. I've still got plenty of mates on the force. I could have you fitted up with anything from a parking ticket to a child molestation charge. Not to mention dealing in dangerous drugs.'

He stood up.

'Right,' he said. 'Now we've got the business out of the way, come and have a look at my paintings. Be as critical as you like. I can take it.'

Sixteen

It was gone two by the time I returned home from the Skindle Musée de Kitsch, and my sensibilities felt as if they were coming down with a bad head cold. I parked my car, locked it and started walking towards my front door. A figure came out of the shadows, hobbling towards me. It was a bent-over old woman with short grey hair, and thick glasses. She wore a shapeless tweed jacket and skirt. Her shoes were thick and clumpy and her woolly stockings bagged at her ankles.

I was about to scream when I noticed she was chewing gum.

'Gut evenink, Mr Garland,' she greeted me, in a hopeless attempt at a mid-European accent.

'Gut evenink,' I greeted her with a stiff nod of my head. 'Doctor Werner, I presume. Look I hate to be a party poop. But I've had a long and terrible night. Can we take a Rhine-cheque on this one.'

'You asshole, Stan Garland,' the woman said, suddenly becoming very New York. 'I've been waiting two fucking hours in that car for you to come home. Now all you can say is you're too tired. You're supposed to be having a relationship with me. You're supposed to care about my wants and needs as well as your own. I need to work out this thing I have with Doctor Werner. I have to do that so I can relate to her properly. I don't want to be stunted. I need to grow as a person. If you care about me, you're supposed to help me. Now get your ass up those stairs. When I ring the bell you answer the door and we'll start from the beginning. One thing.'

'Yes?' I asked wearily.

'Don't be smartass like you usually are,' Maggie Spizer instructed.

Seventeen

I worked out with Australian Fred at the club next morning, having asked him to go easy. He assumed I had a hangover and was sympathetic, signalling his strikes and kicks, allowing me plenty of time for evasions and counters. I had spent a quarter of an hour in my bathroom applying Tiger Balm to my bruises, and it had quickly started a soothing effect.

I was sitting on a bench afterwards, pulling on a warm sweater over my tee-shirt, when Hu Feng came over to me.

'You haven't been to a morning class for a while,' he said.

During the hard exercise and breathing routine he had put us through, he hadn't shown a trace of exertion. Not even working up a light sweat. My tee-shirt was soaked, my limbs were tired, and I felt as if I were the one who was seventy years old.

'I do work out at home every morning,' I protested.

'I'll bet you don't sweat as much as that afterwards. What were you and Fred up to? I don't know what it was, but it wasn't kung fu.'

'I asked him to go easy. I'm a bit sore. I was in a bit of a fight last night.'

Hu Feng looked troubled.

'I hope you weren't engaging in an aggressive act,' he said.

It was one of the rules of membership that none of us should ever use the art in a hostile act against another human being. We could defend ourselves from attack, but never start a fight. If attacked, we should first seek gently to dissuade with something like a wristlock. Only as a last resort should we inflict bodily harm.

'There were three of them and they intended to put me in the casualty ward.'

I didn't tell him that technically I had made the first aggressive move by kicking one of them in the balls. I was two steps back along the Path, but at least I wasn't in a hospital bed.

'I fell over as I delivered a Forward Snap Kick, and they started putting the boot in. Two of them did anyway.'

'Did you go into Drunkard's Stance?' Hu Feng asked with professional interest.

'Yes. It saved me from getting hurt a lot worse. But it was a bit humiliating really. I had to be rescued by a karate black belt who happened to be passing.'

Hu Feng frowned. Like all Masters, he thought his particular form of the martial arts supreme, and karate was way down his list of poor runners-up.

'Karate?' he said, disapprovingly. 'Crude stuff. Most of them get chronic arthritis by the time they're fifty. All that hardening up the hands to chop piles of bricks. What a load of old codswallop. In the Chinese arts it is important to be able to hold a brush as well as a sword. Do karate for a few years and you won't be able to hold a brush in your hand. Let alone paint with it.'

'Funnily enough, this black-belt who helped me out paints. I think you're right about the hands not being able to hold a brush, though.'

We watched Sandra, the stocky nurse, who stood flailing a pair of nuchakas around her body with blinding speed.

'Sandra's very dedicated,' Hu Feng said, approvingly. 'But her attitude lags behind her physical ability. Usually more of a male fault.'

'She scares the shit out of me sometimes. She does it for real. You don't just practise with her. You defend yourself.'

Sandra increased the speed of her whirling. Watching her hurt my eyes but I couldn't look away.

'I'll never be able to do that,' I said.

'Nor can Sandra,' said Hu Feng, pushing me to the ground as the nuchakas slipped out of Sandra's grasp to smash against the wall where I had been sitting.

'How did you know that was going to happen?' I asked, incredulous.

'You develop pre-cognition if you practise these arts long enough,' he said. 'And you keep your hands as soft as a baby's bum.'

I got to my feet and examined the dent in the wall that the

nuchakas had made. Had I been still sitting there, the chances were I would have been a goner.

I left the club more inclined to believe that Hu Feng went astral-tripping.

Eighteen

I was walking back from the former greengrocer's that was now my local health food shop, a carton of soya milk and a loaf of wholemeal bread in my hands, when Captain Midnight's car drew up alongside me. He stuck his head out of the window. His dark glasses reflected a dull, grey sky.

'Your place or mine?' he asked.

'Mine. I haven't had a proper breakfast yet. You wouldn't want me being carsick over your mock-leopard skin upholstery.'

'This is not mock, Babes. This is genuine leopard. Sold to me by a descendant of Zulu kings. Okay, your place. But I can't stay long. Do you want a lift?'

I gauged the twenty-five or so yards that stood between me and my front door.

'I think I'll walk. I need the exercise.'

He drove on, parked, and joined me just as I was fishing around for my keys. The sky darkened. It began to rain. The weatherman had promised sunshine.

'As my old mum might have said, I've got a bone to pick with you,' I said, once we were upstairs.

He held his hands up in a defensive gesture, long, bony fingers splaying open.

'I couldn't help it, Babes. That Skindle is a very heavy guy. He hit me. That freaked me out. Nobody's hit me since I was at school. My body has no resistance to physical assault.'

'All that crap about your great love for Toorey,' I said, annoyed.

Captain Midnight shrugged.

'That was just business, Babes. Nothing personal. It doesn't mean I don't regard you as one of my closest friends. But it was business. You have to bend the truth a little to give yourself an edge. That's the way business operates.'

I filled a bowl with muesli and wheatgerm. I offered some to my guest, but he shook his head. Reaching into the pocket of his white leather jacket, he pulled out the makings and began rolling a joint.

'Isn't it a touch early for that stuff?' I asked. 'You could at least wait until I've had my breakfast.'

'Okay. I'll just get it ready.'

'You're an arsehole,' I said annoyed, pouring soya milk over my muesli and wheatgerm. 'I didn't want to get mixed up with Skindle again. And you went and landed me right in it.'

'I'm sorry. But Skindle really scares me. He also threatened to fit me up with a five year driving ban. I'd die, Babes.'

Behind me a door opened. There was a sound of bare feet padding across to the bathroom. Captain Midnight's head followed the source of the sound until the bathroom door clicked shut.

'There's a little grey-haired old lady just come out of your bedroom,' he said, in a surprised tone. 'I didn't know that was your scene.'

'It's my psychiatrist. She's doing an in-depth study of the things I say in my sleep. She's going to write a paper on it. The Lancet have given her seventy-five thousand quid up front. And I'm still pissed off with you.'

He sighed and shook his head sadly.

'It didn't work out for me, though. Did it, Babes? I'm just not the devious type, at heart.'

I finished off the last few spoonfuls of muesli, then cut myself a slice of wholemeal bread. Captain Midnight watched me.

'I did kind of like Toorey,' he said. 'So I wasn't entirely lying. Oh yeah –' He reached into his white leather jacket again and came out with a slip of paper which he handed to me. 'I got Toorey's address for you,' he said, pleased. 'See. So I was trying to help you. It took me a lot of asking around to come up with that.'

'Terrific,' I said, putting the piece of paper down on the table. 'And you're not getting any of your hundred and fifty back.' I had a sudden thought. 'What about this buyer who got burned along with you. Isn't he going to turn nasty?'

'Skindle already fixed him. He knew him from the old days.

He leaned on him to write it off as a business loss. I don't know what Skindle had on him, but he wore it, in the end.'

'Skindle's got us all jumping through hoops. And we can't do a thing about it.'

'He's a bastard, Babes. One of the original bad guys. Okay if I light up now?'

I nodded and he lit the joint with a lighter he took from a small pocket on his jacket sleeve.

'Can I interest you in a cup of dandelion coffee?' I asked.

'Not right now. But maybe I'll get into it after a few tokes on this joint. Listen, Babes. I think you ought to give me half my bread back.'

'No chance. You owe me that and more for sicking Skindle onto me.'

'But I have nothing, my good fellow. Captain Midnight is penniless. I have to put petrol in the car. The tank is just about empty.'

'No chance,' I said, spooning dandelion coffee granules into a mug.

'You can't do this to me.'

'Want to bet?'

I added a spoonful of Wild Tasmanian Honey and hot water. But when I poured in soya milk, it curdled and I had to throw the whole lot down the sink.

'Listen. How about buying something from me. I've got to have some bread. Any bread. I've got a really nice little dope box. Look.' He reached into another of his pockets and came out with a small brass box that had a little enamelled elephant on top.

'Nice,' I admitted, as he handed it to me for examination. 'Where did you steal it from?'

'It isn't stolen. It sort of belongs to me. Pete dropped it in my car some time. Now he's burned me on the deal, I reckon it's mine.'

'Sounds fair. How much?'

'Fifty?'

'That stuff you're smoking is affecting your brain. Ten.'

'Ten? You're going to pick up a lot of bad karma if you rip me off like this.'

'Twenty. And I'll risk the bad karma.'

I went over to my jacket and found twenty pounds in notes.

'You wouldn't like to make it thirty? I don't think I can fill the tank with this.'

'Drive slower, you'll have a lower fuel consumption.'

He got to his feet.

'There's a very hard side to your nature, Babes. Listen, that little grey-haired old lady who was in here earlier.'

'Yes?'

'I don't know,' he said, shaking his head worriedly. 'I must be getting as weird as you. But that little old lady had a great arse.'

Nineteen

I opened the door of Brian Paxton's office without knocking and almost got my head kicked off by a flying foot. The foot was attached to a large mass of bright pink velour that turned out to be Linda in a training suit. Lying open on the desk was a copy of a woman's self-defence manual, 'Stand Your Ground'. Next to it was a half-eaten sandwich and a cup of coffee.

'Good book,' I said.

'What do you want?' she asked, aggressively.

'Is himself in?' I said, nodding towards the other room.

'He's not in today. His biorhythms are critical. And it is my lunch hour. So why don't you go away?'

I stood my ground.

'Maybe it's you I've got to thank for the visit from Pete's friends,' I said.

'What do you mean?'

'Somebody knew I would be turning up at the Happy Mason and arranged to have some of Pete's mates have a go at me. It could have been quite nasty if things had gone their way.'

'I don't know what you're talking about.'

'It had to be either you or Brian Paxton that tipped them off,' I said.

'Well, it certainly wasn't me,' she said. If I wanted you beaten up, I would be quite capable of doing it myself.'

'I think the self-defence manual is making you over-confident.'

'I belong to a karate club,' she boasted, backing her claim.

'It's getting hard to find anyone who doesn't belong to a karate club these days,' I said wearily. 'Soon they'll be giving black belts away in cornflakes packets. Anyway, I wouldn't have thought you had the time. Being a Friend of the Inner Light is a pretty full-time job, I should say.'

'Ruth encourages us to engage in activities outside the group.

She doesn't believe we should get too enclosed. That's one of the reasons she runs classes for the general public.'

'That, and the money she makes from them.'

'You're a cynical bastard. Just like all pigs.'

'I'm not a copper,' I protested.

'Not anymore you're not. Booted off the force for corruption, wasn't it?' she jeered, angrily.

'Eh? Just a minute. I think you're mixing me up with someone else. I'm not Skindle. He's the one who's the ex-copper. Anyway, he's about twenty years older than me.'

'You're still a bastard, though. All men are,' she added.

'Just a minute, though. How did you get to hear about Skindle? Are you in touch with Pete and Toorey?'

'No.' Her eyes refused to meet mine, and her face was flushed.

'You're lying,' I accused.

'I'm not. Now get out of here.'

'Where are they?'

'I don't know. And I wouldn't tell you if I did.'

'Where are they?' I repeated.

'I don't have to answer your questions. You're not the police or anything.'

'You just said I was.'

'That was before I knew you weren't. Now bugger off before I call the real pigs.' She picked up the phone and looked at me challengingly.

I stood looking back at her. Mike Hammer would probably have ripped the phone from the wall, beaten the truth out of her, laid her a couple of times, then shot her in the stomach. I just turned around and left. I was too soft to be a real private eye.

Twenty

Maurice Willoughby clutched Pete's dope box in his soft, pudgy fingers. Eyes closed, lashes quivering, he began to breathe slowly and deeply. His thinning hair was flecked with grey, I noticed with sad surprise. His forehead was lined with years of small worries, and he wore a dental plate that slipped. I bet Alice Turner, who broke my eleven-year-old heart by choosing 'Moggie' over me, wouldn't be so fast at reaching that decision today, I thought.

Even more so if she knew that 'Moggie' had turned into a forty-year-old weirdo who still lived at home with his mum in a ground floor council flat they seldom ventured out of.

As Maurice carried on with the slow deep breathing, his mother entered, as silent as ectoplasm, and placed two cups of tea on the table. On each saucer there was a chocolate biscuit. When the cups were safely in place, Mrs Willoughby hovered, eyes darting around to see if there was anything else we might need. Satisfied at last that there was not, she departed silently – returning, I supposed, to the pink and green scarf she had been knitting for the last five or so years.

'I'm getting something,' Maurice said, intruding on my thoughts.

'Yes?'

His face was contorted with concentration. There was a light sheen of sweat covering his lined brow. I could hear a clack of knitting needles from the other room.

'It belongs to a man,' he said, still holding Pete's dope box. 'Young, I think.'

'Very good. You're doing fine.'

Maurice concentrated again.

'There's something wrong. Trouble of some sort. Quite bad trouble, I think.'

'That's possible. Where is he? Can you get anything?'

Maurice shushed for me to be quiet and frowned.

'Nothing very clear. Nothing at all, really.'

'Oh well, it was worth a try.'

I dunked my chocolate biscuit in my tea.

'Hold on,' Maurice said. 'I'm getting something. Water.'

'What sort of water?'

'A lot of water. Not the sea. Flowing water. It could be a river. I'm not sure . . .' He stopped, opened his eyes and sat blinking at me.

'Is that it?' I asked.

Maurice looked sheepish.

'I had cheese for lunch,' he admitted. 'Cheese plays havoc with your psychic channels. Buggers up the flow. You get all sorts of blockages.'

'Sounds nasty.'

He brightened as an idea occurred to him.

'You could try Mum,' he suggested. 'She had pilchards.'

Getting up from the chair, he went out to the other room. The needles stopped. Conversation took place. The pair of them came back to where I was sitting.

'It will just be an extra fiver for Mum's reading,' Maurice said. 'I won't charge you the full rate for mine. Not if I wasn't functioning properly. Mum's very good. Better than me, in some ways. After all, that's where I get it all from.'

'Okay,' I agreed. 'An extra fiver.'

Mrs Willoughby gave me a fleeting smile before sitting down in the chair her son had occupied. Her manner became confident, assured and professional. She took Pete's dope box in her hands and concentrated.

'Lots of energy there,' she commented. 'That's good.'

Maurice nodded and smiled at me. I hoped his mother wasn't going to take as long to give me a reading as she took to knit a scarf.

'It belongs to a man,' Mrs Willoughby said. 'A young man. Not a nice young man. Not nice at all.'

'That sounds like Pete,' I said.

'There's money involved. But it isn't honestly come by. There's fear, too. Fear and trouble.'

'Do you know where he is?'

'There's water around him. All around him. Flowing water. A river probably.'

'Is he on a houseboat?'

She shook her head.

'No. Not a boat. Land. But the water is all around him. He could be on an island. He's very worried about something.'

'Where is this river? Do you know?'

Mrs Willoughby opened her eyes and looked at me.

'What do you want with this boy? Do you mean him harm?'

'No. I'm helping someone who's anxious to find him.'

'Stan's alright, Mum,' Maurice assured her. 'He wouldn't consciously harm others. He's a sort of Buddhist.'

'I'm helping his spiritual advisor,' I claimed. 'He's worried about him.'

'Spiritual advisor?' Mrs Willoughby questioned. 'I don't get the feeling of him being a religious sort of boy.'

'He lives with the Friends of the Inner Light.'

'Isn't that strange? I didn't get that feeling about him at all.'

'Hold on,' Maurice said. 'I think they've got a place on the Thames somewhere.'

'Who?' I asked. 'The Friends of the Inner Light?'

'Yes. They run weekend courses there in the summer. It's an island in the middle of the river. Out near Bray somewhere, I think. It shouldn't be too hard to find. There can't be many islands around there.'

I asked Mrs Willoughby if she could read anything else from Pete's dope box, but that was it. I paid Maurice the money, and he walked me to the front door.

'You've got it made here,' I said, standing on the step. 'Tea and chocolate biscuits on tap. Clean shirts and handkerchiefs whenever you need them. Your own special chair to watch telly in.'

'It's not as wonderful as it looks,' Maurice said seriously. 'Mum can be very difficult at times. Still, it's pretty good on the whole.'

'I always meant to ask you. But I always forget. What happened to Alice Turner?'

'I dunno. Her parents moved to Littlehampton.'

'Littlehampton? I didn't know that.'

'Yes. We wrote to each other for a bit. Then I got interested in the Scouts. I didn't bother to write after that. I didn't really like her that much, to tell you the truth.'

'You didn't?'

'No,' he said. 'I only led her on in the first to get at you.'

'Why did you want to do that?' I asked, surprised.

Maurice shrugged.

'You were always taking the piss out of me,' he said. 'I could never think of anything clever to say back. I used to get really hurt. I'd come home and cry my eyes out. That's why I used Alice to get back at you. Seems daft now, doesn't it?'

'It does, I suppose. I'm sorry I took the piss out of you.'

'You still do. You can't help it. It doesn't affect me now, anyway. Stan?'

I turned back.

'Yes?'

'Watch out when you go to this island place. I get some very bad feelings about it. Be careful.'

'I will. Thanks.'

'Stan?'

I turned back again.

'You wouldn't have liked Alice Turner. Not really. Not if you'd really got to know her properly.'

'Vibes again?'

'No. She had this giggle. Did it all the time. It got on your nerves something chronic after a while.'

Twenty-one

Driving through the Oxfordshire countryside, I had an idea for a book. Consisting for the most part of photographs, 'Wildlife on the Roads of Britain', would have lavish illustrations showing squashed, flattened hedgehogs and mutilated birds. There would be close-ups, in beautiful colours, of pheasants dying from the impact of a passing Range Rover. Or rabbits smeared across the macadam by a Mini with humorous stickers in its rear window.

There would be moody shots of a dying sun, its golden rays catching the entrails of a blackbird spilled across the A6453. Dawn on the A3984 would feature carnage reminiscent of a Great War battlefield. I cursed myself for not bringing a camera.

I stopped for lunch at the Jar and Toad. I had a feeling that the publican – a 'Wizard prang' type with a large white moustache and a RAFA tie – was waiting for me to ask him the interesting story behind the pub's name. Instead I ordered a ploughman's lunch and an orange juice and carried them over to a seat by the window.

It was an EEC ploughman's lunch – a measure of dry French bread, a square of butter wrapped in tinfoil, and a small portion of cheese sealed in plastic. By the time I had finished it, I hardly had enough body fuel to make it out to the Gents', let alone work a team of horses and a plough.

Mein Host wasn't entirely sure, old boy, but he thought Waldren on Thames might be the place I was looking for. He charged me fifty pee for the information, in the form of a contribution to the RAFA Benevolent Fund.

I went out to the car park. There were a lot of four-wheel drive cars around. And they all had stickers in their rear windows with demands such as 'Save Our Country Sports' and 'Hands Off Privatisation'. Most of them had green wellies thrown casually in the rear. Probably thrown there for the same reasons that the working class dangle furry dice or baby boots from their rear-view mirrors. As a charm against accidents. I keep a stone I found on a beach in Corsica in my glove compartment. I don't know where this puts me on the social scale.

It was late afternoon by the time I finally found the island. It was about a mile and a half along the towpath leading from Waldren on Thames. As I got there, an early dusk was beginning to fall, bringing a damp mist that quickly chilled me through. There was a small Regency house on the island that had probably been some young buck's weekend place. I could make out a huge curved window facing upriver, and a jetty with a rowing boat moored to a post. But there were no lights.

I wondered if the moored boat meant that there was someone staying at the house. I also wondered how I was going to get over there myself.

I found the answer a little further along the bank, where there were two rowing boats tied up. It took me a while to find the oars to go with the boats; I eventually tripped over a pair in the near darkness. I carried them over to one of the boats and put them in the rowlocks.

The boat rocked dangerously as I pushed off and I fell back onto the seat, jarring my teeth painfully. Up until then my boating experience had been confined to placid, urban park lakes. The river was a different, treacherous place where the current had a will of its own.

Pulling too hard on the right oar, I found myself against the bank again. Pushing off again, I almost capsized. But after a while I got the hang of it, settling into a jerky rhythm.

A pale misty moon came up, thin as a slice of lemon in a glass of pub tonic water. Night creatures called to each other along the banks. Wildfowl, disturbed by my clumsy sculling, screeched across the river's surface. Somewhere behind me a nightingale began running through a series of warming-up exercises. It became colder.

The distant lights of Waldren on Thames beckoned, hinting at untold pleasures centring around warmth and comfort. I was seriously thinking of turning back when the boat banged against the banks of the island.

I had landed some way down from the jetty, but I decided to settle for that. I clambered out and tied the boat to a tree. My white shoes sank heavily into leaf mould. There was a pungent smell of wet earth. Undergrowth almost obscured a track leading towards the house. I took it, trying not to step on dead branches or anything else that might warn of my approach.

Close up, the building looked badly in need of repair. There was a lot of crumbling brick and rotting wood, and several small windows were broken. I took a slow, cautious walk around the outside of the house, looking for any sign of life. There was none.

I arrived back at the front door to stand looking at the jetty in the moonlight. Just along the jetty someone had been splitting logs. The split logs were stacked in piles, suggesting a desire for order that I somehow hadn't associated with Pete. A stump of felled tree had been used as a block for sawing on. The saw, a large silver and blue bow, rested across the stump. There was no sign of the axe, though. I wondered about that. It didn't fit in with the orderly stacks of logs and the saw left to rust in the rain.

A bat streaked out of the shadows to zoom off around the side of the house. It could have just been a trick of the moonlight, I told myself. But I could have sworn the bat was wearing a white shirt front and a black evening cape.

Extending a hand, I cautiously pushed at the front door. It swung open to my touch, with a long, slow creaking sound that had me worrying about the bat again. I cursed myself for having given in to the temptation of smoking a joint while I had sat on the riverbank waiting to see if any lights would go on in the house.

I also cursed myself for not having brought a torch. Flicking on my stick lighter, I saw a small narrow hallway stretching in front of me, with doors leading off on either side. At the far end of the hallway there was a short flight of stairs that I guessed would lead to the room with the large curved window. There was a scuttling sound from the shadows. Mice. Or rats, possibly.

The door to my left led into a tiny kitchen with a calor gas stove in one corner. Most of the remaining space was taken up by a wooden table strewn with the debris of someone's breakfast. There was bacon rind and congealed egg on a willow-pattern plate that had also served as an ashtray. A packet of Sugar Puffs rested on the opened pages of a *Daily Mail*. Making use of the neglected left-hand side of my brain, I checked the date. Yesterday. That probably meant Pete wasn't around. I hoped he wouldn't turn up while I was searching the place for the coke. I was still feeling sore from where his friends had kicked me with their Doc Martin's.

On a shelf over the sink I found a candle screwed into the sort of holder you see in children's story books. I lit the wick and carried the holder across to the room opposite.

It was damper in there. The bedclothes on the iron-frame bed were damp. When I touched the white rough plaster wall, my hand came away wet. There had been a wood fire in the small grate. But not recently. The ashes were cold.

Resting on a shelf across from the bed was a battery-operated portable TV set, and a line of old hardbound books with titles like 'Thrilling Tales for Scouts' and 'The Boy's Book of Adventures'. I had an urge to make a cup of cocoa, light the fire, and curl up in the iron-frame bed with 'Jack Sees it Through'.

I went out into the hallway and along to the stairs at the end. There were double doors at the top of the stairs. Dove-grey with the panel edges picked out in gold. The door handles were gold, too. I ascended the stairs and pushed the doors open.

I hadn't been in a room like this before without being charged an admission fee. I could almost see the young bucks lounging around on the wickerwork chairs and the red and white chaise-longue, bitching about 'Prinnie'. I examined one of the delicately-painted wall panels depicting scenes of Arcadian bliss. They were pleasant enough, but the drawing of the figures suffered from my own weakness: the foreshortening of the limbs left a lot to be desired.

There were quite a few oil-lamps dotted around the room. I picked one up and shook it, hearing a swishing sound that indicated it was nearly full. Removing the glass funnel, I lit the wick and carried the lamp back out to the kitchen. Satisfied that no one was at home, I felt it safe to begin a search for the coke.

The kitchen failed to turn up anything other than someone's addiction to Heinz's Spaghetti Hoops. There were eight tins of them in the food cupboard, arranged in a row along a shelf lined with newspaper. There were a couple of tins of pilchards, one of baked beans and a packet of strawberry jelly. Between the metal chasms of the tinned food, insects fought a grim battle for survival, forming endless food chains and repelling constant attacks in which the victor often devoured the vanquished. Recalling stories of Buddhist monks who welcomed the encounter with a corpse as an opportunity for close study of death, decay and the transitory nature of life on earth, I watched for a while. But in the end I felt sick and had to move on.

Back in the bedroom I went through the plywood wardrobe, but found nothing of interest. There was a guitar under the bed. A Yamaha jumbo. It was better than my own, I decided, after playing a few chords. I put the guitar back in its case and went over to a chest of drawers. There were some tee-shirts and a stack of underpants. Some of the underpants had a picture of a rhinoceros printed on them, with the horn rising in a suggestive manner. But there was no coke.

I went back, sat on the bed and took the guitar out of its case again. It really was a nice instrument, I decided, and wondered if it belonged to Toorey. There were some blank sheets of music paper in the case. I shuffled through them, to see if Toorey had been composing anything recently. Halfway through, I found a birth certificate. It was for the registration of a baby girl born to a Ruth Armstrong in Stratford-upon-Avon in 1953. The girl was called Charlotte Louise. She would be thirty-two now, I worked out. Toorey's age, possibly. The father was unknown.

I put the birth certificate back, replaced the music and the guitar, then went out to the front door to see if anyone was rowing across. Nothing. Just a pair of swans gliding by like ghostly abandoned ships. I went back into the house.

Picking up the oil lamp from the floor, I carried it along the hallway and up into the main room. I was about to begin my search when I noticed something that had escaped me earlier. A door, lying flush with one of the walls, almost invisible except for a small brass handle. I gave the handle a turn and the door opened.

There were stairs leading downwards. I didn't want to go down those stairs. I didn't need Maurice and his mum to tell me the vibes were bad. The smell coming from below was a lot worse than damp. I could hear the skittering again. Mice, I told myself firmly. More strongly than ever, I didn't want to go down the stairs. But I didn't want to have Skindle after me, either. The coke might just be down there somewhere.

I placed a foot on the top step, making the wood creak as it took my weight. I hoped the noise would frighten away whatever was doing all the skittering down there. I continued slowly on down until my feet touched a concrete floor. The smell grew worse. A lot worse. I lifted the lamp and peered around.

The room had once been a boat-house, it seemed. There was the skeleton of a canoe lying in front of me, the fabric long since eaten away by something I didn't care to think about. There were oars stacked against a wall, and bundles of thick rope. There was furniture all over the place – discarded stuff, stacked in careless piles to throw weird, surrealistic shadows in the lamplight.

I found a dressmaker's dummy tipped over onto a battered tin-trunk covered in labels for destinations that for the most part no longer existed. A lifebelt hung from a hatrack. There was a row of tea-chests filled with old clothes and assorted junk. I noticed a bakelite radio similar to the one my parents used to have. I could remember my father checking his football pool results from such a radio. He never won anything. But then, he didn't know anything about football. He didn't care for the game. Or any form of sport for that matter. He lacked a competitive spirit. Maybe that was why he failed to win any of life's prizes.

There were bundles of clothes, picture frames, and a man. The man was lying sprawled across a scattered pile of old 78 records. He had been beaten to death, as far as I could judge. His head and face were covered in deep, purple bruising. Pete, I thought, just before I threw up.

111

When I had finished throwing up, I concentrated on trying to make my legs move again. I willed them to carry me over to the stairs. My heart kept trying to break out of my chest and run on ahead. Using Zen, I became one with the stairs. I became a stair climbing a stair. I tried not to dwell on what I had just seen. I tried hard not to think about the rats crawling over Pete's face. If it was Pete.

Many years on, I arrived at the top of the stairs. I was much older now, of course. What was left of my hair was probably white, I thought. And I moved like an octogenarian in a metal walker. My limbs shook permanently and I didn't think I was ever going to be able to go to sleep again. I wouldn't be able to face the nightmares. I went down the hallway and and kept on going. Skindle and his threats didn't seem that important anymore.

At the front door I blew the lamp out. I breathed deeply, greedily sucking in the cold night air. There was a sound. Oars slapping into water.

A sudden new-found vitality had me running into the shadow of a clump of trees and peering out across the river. There was a boat heading towards the island. One person was aboard. Whether male or female it was impossible to say. All I could tell was that the rowing wasn't any better than mine had been. As the boat drew nearer to the wooden jetty, I stepped back deeper into the shadows.

The boat bumped against the jetty. A figure climbed out. A woman. I caught a sudden glimpse of her face in the moonlight. Toorey. She stood looking towards the house, puzzled apparently by the absence of lights. She called out Pete's name a couple of times. After a few moments of indecision, she started towards the house.

I was about to follow her when a sudden pain cleaved my skull. Lights exploded in my brain. My legs gave way underneath me. The axe, I thought. I'd been hit with the axe. I pitched forward onto the wet compost of dead leaves. The exploding lights disappeared as darkness descended. A definite improvement, was my last thought.

Twenty-two

Pain. Intense pain. Unbearable pain. Become one with it, the voice of the Zen master said. Make friends with the pain. No duality. You are the pain. The pain is you.

I rolled over onto my back and opened my eyes. Above me millions of stars glittered. I had collapsed in an Indian restaurant was my first thought. Then the winking lights of a landing passenger jet told me I was under a night sky.

I rolled over again, manoeuvred myself into a crouching position, then threw up. I suddenly remembered Pete. And the rats. I threw up again.

Putting a hand to the back of my head, I was surprised not to find an imbedded axe. There was a little blood. But nowhere near the amount that the pain merited.

Staying in the crouching position, I crawled over to the river bank and leaned over to scoop water over my face. Encouraged by the small amount of relief that this imparted, I stuck my whole head in the river. A few moments later I was able to climb to my feet, pulling on a tree branch for support.

Once on my feet I forced myself to go through some Liangong breathing exercises. When I felt my Chi was beginning to flow, I ventured a few steps. Not bad. I could walk. Slowly and shakily. All the same, I could do it.

There was a short, heavy length of branch lying near my feet. I picked it up and swung it around experimentally. Not a bad weapon, I decided. Even if the arm muscles weren't up to much at the moment.

I suddenly thought of Pete's killer lurking out there in the undergrowth, while I was searching the house. I shivered. I hoped I wasn't going to find Toorey in the same condition.

Armed with grim forebodings and the branch, I went into the house.

A few minutes later, I was back outside again. There had

been no bogeyman lurking. And no more corpses. Toorey had gone. Along with the killer, I supposed. I wondered if she knew about Pete.

The boat she had rowed over in was still tied up to the jetty. The one that had been there before had gone. On impulse I decided to use it to get back across the river. It would save me a walk of twenty yards or so to the boat I had used before. Not an inconsiderable distance in my present condition.

I was about to push off when something caught my eye. A woman's shoulder bag, wedged down under the wooden seat. Toorey must have taken it off when she started rowing. I picked it up and looked inside.

Lipstick, eyeshadow, a purse containing about seven quid in a mixture of notes and coins, and a ballpoint pen. The only thing of interest was a locker key with the number 124 stamped on its plastic handle. A railway locker, I decided. I put the key in my pocket and replaced the other stuff in the bag. Halfway across to the other shore, I threw the bag into the river. There seemed no point in leaving anything around that might incriminate Toorey in Pete's murder.

It was closing time as I passed the village pub in Waldren on Thames. The locals were squelching their way homewards in their green wellies, scenting the night air with expensive French aftershave lotion. On the whole I was pleased it was past drinking time. The temptation to go inside and down a few stiff vodkas would have been strong.

Arriving back at my car I found a piece of paper trapped in my windscreen wipers. The scouts were running a fifty pee car wash the following morning.

Twenty-three

'Go away,' I protested wearily. 'Just go away.'

'Is that yaw cawr, soir?' the traffic warden persisted, in a hopeless attempt at a cockney accent.

'Piss off,' I said.

The traffic warden bit angrily on her chewing gum.

'Some guys would pay a lot of money for the kind of things I do for you,' she said, reverting to her native tongue.

I found my doorkey and put it in the lock, then summoned up the strength to turn it.

'Look, I've just got in –' I began.

'I know you've just got in, asshole. I've been waiting for you.'

'Why do you have to keep lurking around my house? Why can't you let me know when you're coming? Ring up or something.'

I pushed the door open and switched on the hall light. Maggie watched me speculatively. I was beginning to get into the uniform despite my weariness. Black stockings have been a hang-up for me since my art student days.

'You mean have a date?' Maggie asked, screwing up her face as she thought about it. 'Like a regular couple?'

'Something like that. Yes.'

She nodded to herself, interested.

'Could be kind of kinky,' she agreed. 'I'll try to work it into the schedule.'

'Schedule?' I asked surprised, as she closed the door behind us. 'We're on a schedule?'

'Sure we are. I've worked out a complete programme. Don't ask me what it is, you'll spoil it.'

'Listen,' I said puzzled. 'Supposing I come back here with someone else one night? Another woman. We come back together and you're hanging around dressed as a lady wrestler or Mrs Abe Lincoln or something.'

Maggie shrugged, raising her epaulettes.

'That's okay,' she said. 'I'll improvise. I'm very strong on improvisation. I almost got to be with Second City once. Now are you going to try talk me out of giving you a ticket?'

'Not tonight,' I said, leading the way into my living room. 'I don't think I've got the strength. Anyway, I've got a really bad headache.'

Maggie smiled a slow, evil smile.

'You don't know where I'm going to stick the ticket,' she said.

Twenty-four

Hours later, when Maggie had finally gone to sleep, I climbed softly out of bed. I looked down at her. Her breath rose and fell evenly, jaws working away on phantom gum. It hadn't been easy persuading the traffic warden not to give me a ticket. In the end it had become a point of honour. At least it had taken my mind off Pete for a while.

Going out to the kitchen, I made myself a cup of dandelion coffee and carried it into my living room. The coffee would have tasted a lot better with a large slug of brandy in it, I couldn't help thinking. I debated smoking a pipe of hash, wondering if being stoned could conceivably make me feel any worse than I did at that moment. The phone rang.

It was Skindle.

'Not in bed, were you?' he asked, in a maddeningly jovial manner.

'At half past three in the morning? Never. I was just wondering about toasting some crumpets for tea.'

'Anything to report?'

I sank down onto a large, brightly coloured Indian cushion and rested the back of my head against the wall.

'I managed to find Pete,' I told him.

It had crossed my mind that Skindle himself could have been responsible for Pete's untimely demise. He would be quite capable of beating someone to death. He had both the skill and the downright nastiness required.

'You found him did you? Did he have the stuff?'

'I don't think so.'

'You don't think so?' Skindle said, sounding annoyed. 'What do you mean? Don't start pissing me about, old son. I'll have your guts for a catapult. What did Pete say?'

'Not a lot. He wasn't really in the mood for conversation. Someone had beaten him to death. And there were rats, too.

They were running over what was left of his face.'

'What the fuck are you talking about?'

I sighed and began telling him everything that had happened, including my getting knocked unconscious. The persistent headache was beginning to make me wonder if I should check into a hospital.

'Are you serious?' Skindle demanded, when I had finished.

'I most certainly am.'

There was a moment or two of silence.

'Anyone see you?' Skindle asked, finally.

'No. But there was a pub a few miles away where I asked directions.'

'You stupid nerk. You'll just have to hope the local coppers don't get onto it.'

'Hang on. I didn't kill Pete.' I protested.

'I've managed to secure convictions on less,' Skindle boasted. 'Anyway. It'll probably be alright. Don't go falling apart on me. We've still got a long way to go. This has all come as a bit of a surprise to me.'

'It probably came as something of a surprise to Pete. It's all turning a lot nastier than you led me to believe.'

'It wasn't supposed to,' Skindle assured me. 'There wasn't supposed to be any heavy blokes involved. I was assured we were just dealing with amateurs.'

I could hear the chiming of a cuckoo clock from somewhere behind him.

'Your clock's running slow,' I told him.

'I think we'd better meet,' Skindle said.

'I don't really want to continue this business venture. I think it just moved out of my league.'

'Don't be so modest, Stanley. I'm sure you'll pull through with flying colours in the end. You have to, don't you? Otherwise you'll have me to answer to. We'll have a talk about it all in the morning. Eleven at the King's Castle. That boozer near Camden Lock. I'll ask around my contacts before then. See if I can find out what the fuck's going on.'

He rang off, leaving me listening to the dialling tone. I went back to the kitchen and swallowed paracetamol. One of the tablets caught in my throat, causing a brief, but painful

118

coughing fit. Swallowing water I remembered the locker key I had found.

A railway locker key, I was almost certain. But which one? Euston would be a good bet, with Pete and Toorey being based in North London. Then again Paddington was a possibility. Just the place to stash something if you were catching a train to Waldren on Thames. With the pain in my head making sleep unthinkable, I decided I might as well go and search for the locker now.

I left Maggie talking in her sleep. She seemed to be dreaming some sexual fantasy that involved Stanislavsky and James Dean. Interested, I tried to listen to some of it, but her diction was hopelessly marred by the phantom gum she chewed.

Twenty-five

A chilling mist rolled around under the streetlights. The stars had disappeared. Maybe they had just been in my head. My car didn't like the damp anymore than I did, taking a long time before the engine finally caught. I let it run for a few moments while I smoked an old joint I found in the glove compartment. A modest home-grown variety, but I was amused by its presumption. There was jazz on a Dutch station. Barney Kessel, the announcer identified in perfect English. The home-grown grass was making my head feel worse. I stubbed the joint out in the ashtray. As I moved off, the car stalled. The handbrake was still engaged.

I decided to try Euston first. Vibes. At this hour the place seemed to be populated only by the defeated, the despairing, and the damned. The trains displayed on the indicator board would never arrive. Or leave. The buffet would never open. Nor the mouth of the singing drunk close. Dawn would never dispel the fluorescent lights.

I visited the Gents' to swallow more paracetamol and found a small, exhausted looking man talking to his own reflection in a mirror above one of the washbasins.

'If the folks back in Sydney could see me now, just what the fuck would they say?' he asked.

His reflection didn't reply. It just stared back at him with the same beaten, exhausted expression. Maybe it was tired of hearing him complain. As I left he was pulling at the loose folds of flesh covering his face, as if trying to catch a glimpse of his long-lost youth.

I walked out of the Gents' and along to a row of lockers. When I got to 124, I stopped and looked around to see if anyone was watching me. Satisfied there wasn't, I took out the key and put it in the lock. A perfect fit. Taking another quick look around, I opened the metal door.

There was an envelope inside. About ten by eight and flattish. The wrong shape for holding a kilo of Charley. I took the envelope out, left the key in the lock and started walking away.

Nobody shouted out. Nobody came after me. And nobody hit me over the head with anything. It was all going worryingly well, I thought.

Back in my car, I switched on the interior light and opened the envelope. I took out several strips of 35 millimetre negatives and some blow-up photographs. The photographs featured a naked man and woman in various sexual arrangements. The woman looked out of it on something or other. She was more or less just lying there, having things done to her.

The man was Pete and he seemed to be enjoying himself in a vicious sort of way. I had seen the woman before, too. But only in another photograph. It was Ruth Armstrong from the Friends of the Inner Light.

I put the photographs back in the envelope along with the negatives and stowed them away in my glove compartment. I didn't think I would tell Skindle about this find. I had a feeling I knew how he would use the photographs and I didn't want any part of it.

Driving back I speculated on the birth certificate I had found in the guitar case, wondering if Toorey's real name was Charlotte Louise Armstrong. If it was, the chances were that she was blackmailing her own mother. With pictures of her screwing her daughter's boyfriend. My headache started getting worse.

I called in at the casualty department of a hospital on the way home. I waited a couple of hours or so, along with other victims of the previous night's violence, until I was taken along for an X-ray. As dawn poked its grubby fingers through the slatted blind of his office, a tired duty doctor told me he didn't think there was any real damage. He clearly gave little credence to the story of my banging my head on a table while looking for an I Ching coin that had rolled underneath. I didn't blame him. My powers of invention were not at their best.

He advised me to ease the pain with a couple of paracetamol.

Twenty-six

'Bloody hell. You look a bit rough,' Skindle said, as he joined me at the bar.

'You're three-quarters of an hour late,' I pointed out. 'What happened? Did you run into a jogger's snarl-up coming over Primrose Hill?'

Skindle eased himself up onto the stool next to me. His hard, muscle-packed body was testing the fabric of a grey training-outfit this morning.

'You've got a new romper suit on, I see.'

Skindle brought his ugly face nearer to mine.

'I have warned you about the lip, haven't I, old mate,' he said nastily. 'Get us a Double Diamond. I don't want to break a note and I can't carry change in these clothes.'

A barmaid came along to take my order for a Double Diamond and a Perrier water. Skindle began to piss himself with laughter.

'Coming into a boozer to buy a glass of water. You must be bloody mental. I think that bonk on your bonce must have done you a nasty. It's given you brain damage. Here, darling,' he said, addressing the barmaid. 'What are you going to charge him for his glass of water?'

'Sixty pee.'

Skindle began laughing again, loud enough to attract attention from the other customers.

'Sixty pee for a glass of water?' he gasped. 'I could understand it if you were in the middle of the Gobi desert or something. But in Camden Town –'

'I hope you've got a nappy on under your jimjams,' I said. 'Just in case you wet yourself.'

Skindle turned to the barmaid again.

'What a nerk, eh darling? Still, I suppose you get all sorts in here, being near Camden Lock.'

'All sorts,' she agreed pointedly, as she poured my Perrier water into a glass.

Interpreting her reply as encouragement, proof of his astonishing sexual magnetism, Skindle leaned over the bar.

'How about a nice kiss to start the day?' He asked her.

'You talking to me?' the barmaid asked, as she placed our drinks down in front of us.

'Well, I certainly wasn't talking to him,' Skindle said.

'I'd rather kiss the arse of a dead ferret,' the barmaid said flatly. 'Who's paying?'

I handed her a five pound note, part of my fee from Captain Midnight. It would all be gone soon, I reflected gloomily. Then I would have to start worrying about money again, instead of getting down to some serious painting.

Skindle sat watching the barmaid as she carried my five pound note over to a till.

'Whatever happened to courtesy and civility?' he called after her. 'Don't you want custom?'

'Not your sort.' She looked him over with a contemptuous expression for a moment or two, then asked, 'Where did you get your suit? Mothercare?'

'Careful,' I warned her. 'He doesn't like people giving him lip.'

'Yeah?' she sneered. 'What does he do? Knock them out with his breath?'

'There's nothing wrong with my breath,' Skindle protested, hurt. 'I use a mouthwash, morning and evening.'

'You don't need a mouthwash,' she told him. 'You need drain cleaner.'

She began to walk away. Stopping, as if suddenly remembering something, she turned back.

'I almost forgot,' she said. 'Have a nice day, won't you? And do come back with your friends. They'll always get the same sort of welcome. There, that's your courtesy and civility. Now get stuffed.'

Leaving Skindle bemused, she went off to the far end of the bar to serve another customer.

'What did I say?' Skindle demanded. 'I was only trying to be nice. Most tarts like a bit of a chat-up. She's probably a bloody les or something. Here – He leaned over and blew malodorous breath into my face. 'Does my breath really smell?' he asked, concerned.

'They could put it in canisters and use it to break up demo mobs,' I told him.

Skindle looked depressed.

'I thought the mouthwash would do it,' he said gloomily.

'I'm afraid you've got a social problem on your hands. Maybe you should write to one of the agony aunts. "Dear Virginia Ironside, I am an ex-policeman forced into an early retirement by an internal inquiry board. I am still vigorous and anxious to have relations with the opposite sex –"' I stopped as a wave of sudden, excruciating pain swamped my thigh. I looked down to see Skindle's thumb pressing into a nerve centre.

'Lip,' he identified. 'I warned you about it.'

He took his thumb off and some of the pain went away.

'Have you managed to find out anything?' I asked, reverting to our business relationship, as I rubbed at my thigh with the palm of my hand.

'Nothing. I don't understand it. I've asked around and there's no one else involved. It sounds like some bloody amateurs have come into the picture. They're bad news. Unpredictable. They do things like killing that stupid sod Pete. You sure he was dead?'

I told him about the rats again.

'Might turn out to be a bit of luck for you,' he said, when I had finished. 'If no one finds him for a bit, they'll have eaten most of the evidence.'

'What do you mean? I didn't kill him.'

'Ah, but you could have done. If I was an investigating officer, I would have to hold you on suspicion. Bloke beaten to death. Another bloke on the scene who studies the martial arts. Open and shut case.'

'What about you?' I protested. 'I'm not convinced that you didn't do it. You've got the motivation and you practise karate.'

'Bollocks,' Skindle dismissed this, unconcerned. He took a long swallow from his glass, then turned back to me. 'You didn't find anything there at all?'

'Nothing. Unless you count Pete.'

Skindle stared at me thoughtfully, making me wonder if he somehow knew about the locker key.

'You wouldn't try anything funny with me, old mate, would you? I could turn very nasty indeed if I thought you were going into business for yourself.' He shook his head dismissively. 'No,' he said. 'You haven't got the bottle for anything like that.'

'Quite right,' I agreed. 'So, if it's all the same to you, I would like to pull out at this stage.'

'Oh no,' Skindle said quickly. 'Not yet, old son. There's too much cash involved. You're going to go on until you find Toorey for me. And she'd better have the Charley. If she turns out to have the cash they got from burning that dealer as well, I'm prepared to give you a bonus. I'll up your fee to two thousand quid. That'll buy you a lot of artist's models.'

'I don't work from life anymore.'

'Never mind, you'll think of something to do with the money. Order us up another Double Diamond, will you? I've got a thirst on. Must be the vicarious excitement of hearing about you being hit over the head with the traditional blunt instrument.'

I attempted to attract the attention of the barmaid, who stood further down the bar reading a newspaper. Skindle took over.

'Come on, darling,' he called out. 'You do work here, don't you?'

The barmaid folded her newspaper. Slowly and carefully. When eventually she had finished, she consented to walk over to us.

'Haven't I seen you before somewhere?' she asked Skindle, feigning a sudden interest.

'I don't know,' he murmured, uneasily.

'I'm sure I have.' She snapped her fingers. 'Of course. In my mum's front garden. You were pushing a little wheelbarrow. And you were wearing a floppy red hat and curly-toe shoes.'

'You're a sour cunt,' Skindle told her. 'What's the matter? Doesn't your husband give you enough?'

'Plenty, thanks. But he can always spare a bit, if your wife needs some. He's very keen on helping the underprivileged.'

'That's enough,' Skindle cautioned sternly.

'Ooh,' the barmaid gasped, shuddering and fluttering her eyelids. 'I just love strong, masterful men. They make me come all over queer. I shall have to go and lie down.'

'Silly cow,' Skindle commented, watching her long, slim legs as she went away to get our order.

'Nice legs,' I said.

'Too skinny. I like tarts with a bit of meat of them.' He slipped down off the stool. 'Bring the drinks over to the table. We'd better work out what you're going to do.'

He started for a table, changed his mind and headed towards the Gents'.

'Is he a friend of yours?' the barmaid asked, puzzled, as she brought our drinks.

'No,' I replied. 'He's my probation officer. He wants to put me back inside. I'm trying to talk him out of it.'

She looked sympathetic as she took my money.

'I should get your girlfriend to go out and buy a packet of cake-mix and a file. He looks a heartless bastard.'

I carried the drinks over to a marble-topped table where Skindle sat doing simple tricks with a couple of beer mats.

'You been through Toorey's flat yet?' he asked.

'Not yet. I'm not very good at breaking and entering.'

'Well, I reckon you'd better get round there. I doubt if she's got the stuff there. But you never know.'

Holding out a couple of his brutal-looking fingers, Skindle attempted to balance the beer mats on them. After several unsuccessful attempts, he gave up.

'I knew a bloke who could balance four at once,' he told me. 'One on each finger. He could do it with both hands at the same time. He learned to do it when he was doing a stretch for receiving stolen goods. Gave him something to show for his time.'

'Very commendable. There's something to be said for the penal system after all.'

Skindle threw the beer mats onto the table.

'Right,' he said. 'I think it's time you pulled your finger out. I want that Charley. And I want it a bit sharpish. I suspect you're

126

the sort of bloke who needs a challenge to bring out the best in him. I'll expect you to have some good news for me tomorrow night. That gives you long enough to come up with something or other. Go round to that Toorey tart's place, see if you can get any idea where she's pissed off to. I've got Captain Midnight keeping his earholes open. If he finds out anything, I'll pass it on to you. But I want some results.'

'I don't think I'll be able to deliver them.'

Skindle leaned in towards me.

'Oh, I think you'll be able to come up with something. The right hand side of my brain tells me you're holding something back. I think all this psychic stuff must be catching. I'll be home tomorrow night. It's my television night. The missus goes off to bingo. You give me a bell. Let's say by nine. I shall expect to hear you've made a lot of progress.' He stifled my protests with a wave of his hand. 'Drink up, old son,' he advised. 'You haven't got a lot of time to waste.'

Twenty-seven

There were three bells alongside the front door of Toorey's house, but none of them brought a response. Bending over, I peered in through the letter box and saw a small collection of mail lying on the floor. Brown envelopes mostly. I let the metal flap fall back as I stood up again. There was a note tucked into one of the milk bottles standing on the door step. A minor classic of short story writing, it read, 'One pint only from now on, please'. I stood toying with the various plots suggested by the note until I became aware of a woman across the street looking at me.

She sat directly opposite, framed in a window, her elbows resting on a cushion on the sill. Placed within easy reach there was a steaming cup of tea. As I walked over, she picked up the cup and began sipping, awaiting my arrival with mild interest.

'Good morning,' I began.

'Not bad,' she granted, with a nod of her head. 'Though strictly speaking it's afternoon now.'

Up close she was a Picasso giantess with enormous limbs and huge swollen breasts. Rising from the grotesque distortion of flesh was the face of a plastic doll – pink and smooth, with eyes the colour of a tranquilized elephant. She could have been twenty-five or fifty-five. I found it impossible to tell.

'Good afternoon then,' I said, trying to get our relationship on a better footing.

'It's alright,' she conceded, with a gracious nod of her head that reminded me of the Queen Mother. 'Though they do say as how it's going to piss down later. Not that I give a bugger. I'm not going anywhere. Veins,' she explained enigmatically.

'You spend a lot of time here?'

'Most of the time I'm awake. I have trouble sleeping. It's probably all the tablets I take. What are you after, then? Are you on the earhole from some charity or other? Or are you selling something?'

'Neither.'

'If you've got any give-away offers or free trial packages, I'll take them off your hands.'

'I'm not a salesman.'

'No. I didn't think you was.'

She raised the cup to her lips again and sipped her tea, keeping her little finger crooked.

'What are you, then?' she asked, as she set the cup back down again. 'A burglar? I noticed you trying all the doorbells over at that house. You're wasting your time there. Pretty poor pickings. The ground floor flat's wife has just buggered off because she's sick of him being on social security. Terrible quarrels they had.' She smiled reminiscing. 'Terrible. You could hear them right across the street. Every word.'

'That must have been awful for you,' I commiserated.

'Shocking. Nicely spoken couple, too. Even when they were effing and blinding at each other, their diction was crystal clear. I wouldn't be surprised if they'd had professional training.'

'The wife wasn't the one who was a folk singer was she?'

The Picasso giantess rested her gaze on mine.

'What's your game, then?' she asked.

'Skindle,' I confided in a low voice. 'Detective Sergeant Skindle of West End Central.'

'Bollocks,' the Picasso giantess said. 'You're not a copper. You haven't got any authority about you.'

'How about the press?'

'Better,' she granted, with her gracious nod.

'She's won a newspaper competition. Ten thousand quid in cash. We're trying to trace her so we can present it to her.'

'What competition?'

'In the *Daily Mirror*. You had to guess the combined weight of the Royal Family. Toorey Dunphee got nearest – three hundred and four tons. Actually, it's three hundred and fifty six tons if you count third cousins.'

'Bollocks,' she said again. 'What are you really after her for? You from the HP? If you're after her for money, you're out of luck. She's done a bunk.'

'Yes?'

'I saw her go, didn't I? A moonlight flit. I haven't seen one of them for years. Probably owes a few months rent.'

'How long ago?'

'Week or so. You won't find her now.' She laughed, displaying genuine pleasure. 'Not a chance. Two big suitcases she had. And a couple of guitars. I suppose she was buying them on instalments. I've no time for people who get things on the never-never, then find they can't afford them. Living beyond their means.'

'How did she go? Taxi?'

The Demoiselle de Chalk Farm raised a sausage shaped finger and thumb in a gesture as old as time.

'What's it worth to you?' she asked, rubbing the finger and thumb together meaningfully. 'It wasn't a taxi. I could give you a description of the bloke who picked her up in his car.'

'Young bloke. Short, muscular. I know.'

'No. Not him. Though I have seen him over there a lot. I'm talking about another bloke. It must be worth a tenner to you. Your firm can run to that, can't they?'

'How about a fiver?'

'Tenner,' she insisted, in a manner that curtailed any further negotiations.

I pulled a tenner out of my top pocket and gave it to her.

'Not much cop at bargaining, are you?' she sneered. 'I was prepared to come down to seven fifty.'

I watched my money vanish away into a pocket of her floral apron.

'So, what did he look like?' I asked, impatiently.

Sure of my interest, the giantess began to do such maddening things as stir her tea and toy with straying ends of her hair. Twice she teased me by making a show of being about to speak and then suddenly turning the gesture into a yawn. I was on the point of reaching through the window for her throat when she gave me a description of the man she had seen collecting Toorey in his car.

'If you've got another tenner, I'll tell you something else,' she said.

I reached into my top pocket again and handed her the money.

'Your flies are undone,' she told me.

'Thanks.' I zipped them up and began to walk away.

'I'll tell you something else,' she said, stopping me. 'There was two other blokes round here asking about her. Little coloured bloke with a bald head and a grey moustache. And a white bloke. Big feller. Well over six foot. Long ginger hair, going a bit thin on top. Mean anything to you?'

'Not a lot,' I said. 'Is that going to cost me another tenner?' She laughed.

'No,' she said. 'You can have that on the house. You're a good customer. The other blokes wouldn't come up with more than a fiver.'

Twenty-eight

The kid in the glass-fronted booth was singing about life on the road. He made it sound good. He left out stuff like being stuck in sleeting rain on a cold Sunday highway, with a dollar and ten cents in your pocket and a temperature of 103. That had happened to me once in my short stint as a folk singer in the US. All the same, by the time the kid was a couple of choruses in, I was ready to try the whole thing again. When he came to the end of the song, he did some nice fancy embellishments on the upper frets of his guitar.

'Okay Don, that was a good one. We'll play it back to you over the cams.'

Brian Paxton swung around to face me as the engineer sitting beside him began pressing various buttons. There was a notice above them that warned drugs were banned on the premises. Paxton was annoyed.

'I told Linda not to let anyone know I was here,' he snapped. 'I was only to be contacted in a matter of extreme urgency.'

'Don't blame her. I talked to her on the phone. I said I was from the HP company, and we were coming to repossess your car. I was pretty convincing. I used a Scots accent. That always gives it a lot more menace.'

'My car isn't on the HP,' Paxton said. 'I never have anything on credit. I would have thought Linda would know that about me.'

'You haven't heard me on the phone. I need to have a talk with you.'

'Not now. I'm in the middle of a recording session with a client. Come and see me in the office tomorrow.'

'No. I want to talk to you now.'

'I don't like your attitude.'

'I'm not auditioning it,' I said with a mental nod to Philip Marlowe. 'Where's Toorey? I know you took her away in your

132

car the night she was supposed to have disappeared without trace from the Happy Mason.'

Paxton glanced worriedly at the sound engineer. But he was off in that special place sound engineers occupy when they work. Headphones covering his ears, his face wore a contented expression that would have taken me ten years hard in a Zen monastery to attain.

Paxton got out of his chair and led me out into the hallway. We walked as far as a lounge area, equipped with a drink-dispensing machine and a couple of tacky-looking chairs.

'Just who are you? And what do you want?' Paxton demanded, with an aggression that failed to mask worry.

'Someone who needs to find Toorey. A bit sharpish. If I don't find her, there's a man leaning on me. A very nasty man who could make my life a misery. I don't want that to happen. If that means I have to beat the information I want out of you then I'm prepared to do it.'

'Don't go butch on me,' Paxton begged. 'I can't stand it when people get butch with me.'

Suddenly losing patience, I grabbed a handful of his white roll-neck sweater and banged him against the drink-dispenser. The impact set the mechanism of the machine in motion, producing a rumbling sound that was followed by the click of a plastic cup falling into place.

'My arse,' Paxton shrieked, as a squirting noise started up. 'It's scalding my arse.'

I held him tighter against the machine.

'Where's Toorey?' I asked again.

'The pain. I can't stand the pain. Stop.'

'Where's Toorey?'

'My arse. I can't stand it. I can't stand it.'

Breaking from my grip, he flung himself away from me. His hands went to his buttocks.

'Look what you've done,' he said tearfully. 'I'm bleeding.'

He showed me the red stuff covering his hands.

'That's tomato soup,' I told him.

'I'm in agony,' he wailed, dabbing at the soup that covered his trousers. 'You sadist. I hate pain. I loathe it. It isn't my thing at all. My poor arse.'

'If you don't tell me what I want to know, I'll boil your goolies in hot chocolate. What's going on with you and Toorey? And before you give me any bullshit, I've got the photographs and the negatives.'

'What photographs?' he asked, still dabbing gingerly at his rear.

'The ones of Pete screwing Toorey Dunphee's mother in your office. I recognized it from the Utrillo reproduction on the wall in one of them. It took me a while, but then I remembered where I had seen it.'

'I have no idea of what you're talking about. Pete screwing Toorey's mother? In my office? Are you on drugs or something?'

The drinks-dispenser growled in a threatening way. It didn't seem to like Brian Paxton anymore than I did. Maybe it had been a night-club act in a previous life.

'Come off it, Paxton,' I told him. 'I saw the photographic equipment in your office when I was there.'

'I keep that for taking promotional pictures for my clients. It can save a fortune. But I certainly don't go in for pornography. Just what are you going on about?'

I had an awful feeling that his protests of innocence were genuine.

'Could Pete and Toorey have had access to your office?' I asked.

He hesitated.

'I let Toorey sleep there a couple of times,' he said. 'When she had nowhere to live. Before she had enough money to rent a room. That was two or three months back. Before work started picking up for her.'

It could have been then I thought. Toorey had the key, and the photographic equipment was there. Maybe Paxton was in the clear on that one. But there was something else.

'You were seen collecting Toorey from her place on the night she vanished. The night she and Pete vanished with a kilo of coke and the twenty-five thousand quid they got paid for it. Are you in on the deal with them?'

'I didn't know it was anything to do with that amount of money. Toorey told me she had got into some trouble with a couple of small-time dealers and she needed to disappear for a few days. Just until tempers cooled off a little. I know she takes heroin. I've been trying to persuade her to kick it. Though she does seem to have it under control.'

'You're a very understanding sort of agent.'

Paxton hesitated.

'Well,' he said. 'Toorey's a little different.'

'Yes?'

'Yes. You see, she might be my daughter. A youthful indiscretion, I'm afraid.'

Twenty-nine

I bought us both a cup of coffee from the dispenser. And Brian Paxton told me about his youth. Or some of it. It was only with difficulty that I managed to stop him from starting with his first moments on leaving the womb. He had been working in a record shop by day and playing in a skiffle group by night when he met Ruth Armstrong. The skiffle group played in a coffee bar popular with students, and she turned up there one night with a crowd of her fellow medical students. Paxton had only been dabbling with homosexuality at the time, and he and Ruth had been attracted to each other. Following a few dates, they ended up in bed together. Paxton didn't enjoy the experience much. If anything, the physical expression of the attraction he had felt for Ruth disgusted him.

His disgust did not go unnoticed. They quarrelled. Ruth did not take kindly to his explanation of latent homosexuality. As a punishment for either him or herself, she spent the next couple of weeks laying just about every man in the coffee bar. Within a month she was pregnant.

She claimed not to know whose child it was. By this time Paxton guessed that she wasn't really playing with a full deck. She took to wearing clothes that emphasized her condition and to turning up at the record store where he worked by day, and at the coffee bar where he played guitar at night. Sometimes she would ring him up at work and taunt him by naming all the possible contenders to paternity of her child. The list became longer and more fanciful. Several Hollywood film stars appeared on the list. By this time Paxton had had his fill. He told her to fuck off and never bother him again.

To his surprise she took his advice. She didn't ring him at work anymore. And she no longer came to sit at one of the front tables in the coffee bar. Someone told him she had had her baby and immediately had it fostered. Someone else told him she had gone abroad, to the East, and taken her baby with her. Years later, he heard about her starting the Friends of Inner Light. He didn't know what had happened to the child. All that he knew was that it had been a girl.

Toorey turned up at his office by chance. She had been singing around the clubs for several years, and someone had suggested she find herself an agent. Paxton listened to her sing, saw the potential and took her on. He didn't think her name – Charlotte Louise Armstrong – was right. He rechristened her Toorey Dunphee. She seemed grateful to him. She hadn't really felt right about her former name.

When Paxton learned that Toorey had been brought up in care, he became concerned. Perhaps, after all, this was his daughter. It was possible. He told Toorey the story, but she didn't seem that interested. He sensed that she bore a deep and bitter resentment towards her parents. Wisely, Paxton thought, he let the matter drop. But he couldn't forget that he might be her father.

'A little late to start a father-daughter relationship, you might think,' he said. 'But I do have this feeling towards her. I can't help it. I care deeply about her. No matter what kind of trouble she's got herself into. Although I would think Pete would be the one to blame. He really is an awful person. I'm sure she could do better. Is there going to be trouble for her?'

'Maybe,' I said. 'Skindle's a nasty sod. Especially when he smells money. If she turns the coke over to him, it'll probably be alright.'

'It's not so much Toorey not wanting to hand it over, I worry about. It's Pete. He does like to show he's tough.'

'Don't worry about Pete,' I told him.

He raised his eyebrows and simpered.

'Now who's being all tough and macho. You think you can handle him, do you?'

'I'm sure of it. Where can I find Toorey?'

'I don't want anything to happen to her. I love her. In my funny, queer old way.'

'She's a long way from being Snow White. Toorey has been trying to blackmail her own mother, from what I can guess.'

'I know,' he conceded with a sigh. 'She's a junkie. And she's capable of doing terribly cruel things. But it's not entirely her fault. She did have terrible parents – a poofter and a lunatic. And both of them abandoned her. Not much of a start in life.'

'I suppose you're right. I'll do what I can to stop anyone hurting her. Where is she?'

He hesitated.

'I'll just have to trust you, I suppose. There's a friend of mine. A theatrical costumier. Poor old Ron is having a spot of financial trouble at the moment. He might have to close down. He's not using his premises at the moment, so I borrowed his key. Toorey's hiding out there. Try to stop them hurting her, won't you?'

'I'll try,' I told him, hoping I could get to her before Skindle did, or even worse, the person who had found Pete. 'I'll try.'

Thirty

As I left the recording studio and started for my car, two men fell into step either side of me. One was a short West Indian, with a shaven head and a grey moustache. The other was white, tall and heavily built. His hair was ginger, and I guessed it would be going thin on top.

'Show him, Roy,' the ginger-haired man directed his companion.

The West Indian man moved the camel-hair coat he had thrown over his shoulders to reveal a gun pointed at my navel.

'Okay?' the ginger-haired man asked me.

'Fine.'

'Of course,' the ginger haired man began again in a friendly manner. 'You could be the victim of a hoax. Roy could be showing you one of those clever Japanese reproductions. Very hard to tell from the real thing. Even for an expert.'

'I'm no expert,' I told him. 'I'll go for the gun being the real thing.'

The man nodded approvingly.

'A wise choice on balance,' he said. 'I can see we are dealing with a man who is not cut from the common cloth. Eh, Roy?'

'Unlike his suit,' Roy said, his free hand fingering the lapels of my jacket with mild disgust. 'Where did you get these inferior threads, man?'

'C & A. I don't wear suits often. It seemed daft to spend a lot.'

They walked me over to a car, a silver Mercedes saloon with tinted windows. Roy and I got in the back, while the ginger-haired man slid in under the wheel.

'Where are we going?' I asked.

'Roy's place,' the ginger-haired man told me, seeming surprised that I didn't know. 'Just off Ladbroke Grove. He runs a club there – the Pink Pineapple. Nice place. He's got this very quiet room out in the back. We're going to have our little talk there.'

'Talk?'

'That's what you'll be doing. We'll be listening.'

'Are you sure you've got the right bloke?' I asked.

'Not entirely,' the ginger-haired man admitted, with a candour I might have found winning under different circumstances. 'But I think we're in with a good chance of it being you. Our paths keep crossing. You were round at Toorey's place this morning. Now you're seeing Paxton –'

'How did you know I was at Toorey's place this morning?' I asked, surprised.

'The old bag opposite. We dropped her a few quid to ring us up if anyone else called round to see her. She gave us quite a good description of you on the whole. Wouldn't you say, Roy?'

'Pretty good. Though I wouldn't say his nose was that big.'

We drove until we came to a side-street off Ladbroke Grove. Most of the buildings around were boarded up, and the one or two shops still holding on had heavy metal grilles covering their windows. The street itself was littered with the products of a consumer society – takeaway-food containers, soft-drink cans, rusting abandoned cars, discarded furniture. It was the sort of area where the roadsweepers went around in twos.

We stopped alongside a lilac door with a pink pineapple painted on it. There was a man leaning against the door, smoking a cigarette. He was very large and very black. His white chef's jacket was tightly stretched over the sort of muscles you see in a Marvel comic. When we were out of the car, the ginger-haired man seemed quite small beside him.

As we filed in through the lilac door, the man in the chef's jacket flipped his cigarette away and followed us. I found it increasingly hard to think positive thoughts, as some of my self-improvement books suggested for such situations.

We walked through a large room arranged with red and white check-cloth tables. There was a small area for dancing and a stage at one end. We walked as far as the stage, then veered left through a bamboo curtain, and entered a door marked 'Private'.

The man in the chef's jacket followed us in. I had been

hoping he would stay outside.

'I was hoping you'd stay outside,' I told him.

'This is Eddie. Eddie Kingston,' Roy introduced him. 'One of the most promising heavyweights anyone ever saw. He could dance around like Nureyev and hit like a steam-hammer. Then things went wrong for him. Eddie isn't too smart. But he sure knows how to hurt people.'

I waited for him to elaborate on what had gone wrong for Eddie, but he failed to do so. I thought it better not to ask. I believed the part about Eddie being good at hurting people.

'Right,' the ginger-haired man began briskly, turning around from sliding the bolt on the door. 'I don't know about you. But I, for one, am sick of gratuitous, meaningless violence. It bores the tits off me. If I see another boot go into someone's balls, I'll scream out loud with boredom. Do you agree?'

'I think so,' I said, cautiously.

'Good. I'm glad to hear it. Because you'll be pleased when you hear what we're going to do.'

'What are we going to do?' I asked, anxiously.

'We are going to play a little game. Just like you see on the telly.'

'Is Eddie going to play?'

'He is, indeed.'

'I don't think I'm going to like this game.'

'Now, now. You mustn't start with a negative attitude. Right. I am going to be your genial host. Your questionmaster. Roy here will be the strictly impartial jury who decide if you are telling the truth.'

'What does Eddie do?'

'If the strictly impartial jury decide you're not telling the truth, Eddie knocks you around a bit.'

'What happens if the strictly impartial jury decides I am telling the truth?'

'Eddie may still knock you around a bit. It depends on how we feel about what you tell us. Good news or bad news. Like in the old days. When some poor sod risked his bollocks to get a message to the king, only to have his eyes plucked out because he told the old bastard his shares had dropped or something.'

Eddie slowly turned his massive head to spit on the floor. If

Roy minded him spitting on the floor of his office, he didn't say anything. I didn't blame him. Eddie was a very frightening person.

'How hard do you want him hit?' Eddie asked, as his head came back round again. His voice rumbled deep as an Underground train. 'Do you want him hit hard, soft, or medium? Or do you want him hit real hard?'

'Just a light tap for the first few questions,' the ginger-haired man said, giving me a pleasant smile. 'Those will just be the easy ones. The sort everyone can get right.'

I sized up my chances. It took a fraction of a second to work out I was in for a beating unless they liked what I told them. I wondered if Eddie had been responsible for Pete's battered head.

'Right,' the ginger-haired man said in a breezy manner. 'First question for our first contestant. And what is your name, sir?'

'Stan Garland,' I mumbled, embarrassed by his insistence on playing the ridiculous game.

'Stan Garland,' he announced, turning to an imaginary audience. 'True or false? What does our completely impartial jury think?'

Roy looked dubious.

'I don't know,' he said, doubtfully. 'It came out kind of glib. I don't know –'

'The clock is ticking away,' the ginger-haired man cautioned him. 'I'm afraid I'm going to have to hurry you on this one.'

Roy made up his mind.

'We'll give him the benefit of the doubt.'

'Alright. Next question. What is your normal occupation?'

'I'm a painter,' I mumbled again, wishing he would stop.

'House, sign, or mad artist?'

'Mad artist.'

'Hit him, Eddie,' the strictly impartial jury instructed.

'It's true,' I protested. 'You can check. I've got some paintings in a gallery in Camden Town.'

Eddie shuffled around in front of me.

'Just a tap,' the strictly impartial jury advised.

I moved just ahead of the blow to my gut and let it sail past me, using an evasion technique learned by many hours practice in class. But I couldn't stop the one that rapped me around my ear.

'Nicely judged, Eddie,' I heard Roy say, as I covered up against another attack. 'Fast, too. You've still got the old touch.'

'I think he understands the game now,' said the ginger-haired man, as Eddie relaxed again. 'Let's move onto the harder questions. Here we go with one of the Star Prizes. Get this one right, and Eddie doesn't hit you in the gut with one of his hard punches.'

'I don't want him to do that,' I said, rubbing my ear.

'It's a prize worth having then, isn't it? Here comes the question. Where is the Charley?'

'I don't know.'

There was a nasty silence that was finally broken by a soft chuckle from Roy.

'Shit,' he said. 'This man is just a sucker for punishment. Maybe he's one of them masochists you hear about.'

'Very strange,' the ginger-haired man agreed. 'Let's just give him a go at the second Star Prize question. Then Eddie can put a one-two combo together. Where is Toorey Dunphee?'

'I don't know,' I found myself saying.

Roy began chuckling to himself again. I could hear an electric guitar tuning up in the other room.

'Alright,' said the ginger-haired man in a reasonable tone. 'We'll come back to that one as well. Third time lucky perhaps. Where's Pete?'

He waited.

'And a breathless hush has come over the audience,' he began again. 'Is the contestant going to answer? And if he does, will it be the right answer? Or the right-hook? His lips are moving. He's going to speak.'

'Pete's probably where you left him,' I said. 'He didn't look as if he was about to go anywhere. Not after Eddie had got through with him.'

'Eh?' the ginger-haired man questioned, dropping the genial quizmaster manner.

'Did Eddie just get over-enthusiastic? Or did he mean to kill him?'

'Are you telling us someone's knocked off Pete?' Roy asked, worried.

'I found him. He'd been beaten to death by someone who could hit hard.'

'Not Eddie,' Roy denied. 'He only hits the guys I tell him to. I didn't turn him onto Pete. We don't even know where he is. We've been looking for him.'

'This is getting heavy,' the ginger-haired man said. He turned back to me. 'You're not pissing us about, are you? he asked.

'I wouldn't dare. Eddie scares the shit out of me.'

I elaborated on the information, telling them about the place on the island, and how I had found Pete. I left out the part about Toorey showing up there, but I made a lot about getting hit over the head. I failed to elicit much sympathy from my audience.

'Shit,' Eddie said, in a low voice that had the windows rattling. 'I never let no dude take me from behind. I'd feel him coming. Ain't nobody ever take me from behind. Not from behind. Not from the side. Not from the front. Ain't nobody ever take me from no place.' His Muhammad Ali tirade stopped suddenly, and he continued in a quieter, sadder tone. 'Leastways they wouldn't have. Not if things hadn't gone wrong for me—'

He tailed off and just stood there, in the fighting crouch he had unconsciously adopted. His eyes were moist and clouded with old sorrow.

'Sure Eddie,' Roy's voice broke in softly, after a while. 'You were special. A one-off. They broke the mould when they got through making you. You were truly beautiful. If things hadn't gone wrong for you, maybe you could have been the greatest ever.'

He reached out with his balled fist and touched Eddie gently and lovingly on his huge chin. He turned back to me.

'Where's the coke?' he asked.

'I haven't got it and I don't know where it is. Honest. Eddie can beat me into garden compost but you'll still get the same answer.'

Roy stared at me long and hard.

'What do you think?' he asked the ginger-haired man, after

what seemed a couple of hours.

'For some funny reason I believe him. I don't think he does know.'

Roy nodded in agreement.

'Yeah. Me too,' he sighed. 'We're still in trouble with Skindle.'

'Skindle?' I questioned sharply. 'You wouldn't be speaking of ex-Detective Sergeant Skindle late of West End Central, would you?'

'You know him?' Roy asked.

'I know him.'

I left some half an hour later, and by then we were all on first name terms. Even Eddie and I were getting along. Though I despaired of his humour – constant lightning rights that stopped a half inch from my solar plexus. It turned out that Skindle had something on both Bill, the ginger-haired man, and Roy. And he had been using them in much the same manner as he had me. Bill had been given till Monday to come up with the coke. Roy had almost a week left. The two of them had met up when independently questioning the Picasso giantess.

They both commiserated with me for having drawn the earliest of Skindle's deadlines. Then Eddie showed me to the lilac door. He complimented me on my evasion techniques and asked if I'd done any fighting. I told him I studied kung fu. But it would be a long while before I'd care to go up against him bare-handed. I'd need to even things up with something like a pair of nuchakas.

Then suddenly I had an idea of how Pete might have met his death. A pair of nuchakas, used by someone who knew how to handle them, could have caused that kind of damage. It wouldn't need much physical strength. Just skill.

A woman could have done it.

Thirty-one

There were no lights showing in the windows of the 'Dressing-up Box'. The notice in the door, announcing that the premises were closed, looked as if it had been there a long time. But the amusement arcade next door was doing great business, deafening me with a neurotic mélange of clanging machinery, electronic bleeping and Top Ten hits. I tried the handle of the door a few times, but it was locked. I stepped back and winced as the blast from the amusement arcade hit me, then walked over to the alley running alongside the building. Halfway along I found a side-door. It was open.

I had brought a torch this time. If I could have laid my hands on a safety-helmet, I would have brought that along, too. Turning my awareness onto maximum, I stepped into the doorway, telling myself that nobody was going to take me from behind, the side or the front. If I had been Eddie's size, I might have had more confidence in my boast.

I switched on the torch. In front of me a group of ladies wearing dusty bonnets and crinolines were frozen in silent conversation. They were watched by a Hussar with no arms. Behind them were long racks of period clothes and cardboard boxes overflowing with things like button shoes and lace gloves. Unnerved by the glassy stares of the figures, I forced myself to go over and make sure they were not real. Satisfied, I moved on.

There was a steady pounding coming from the amusement arcade next door, and the neon lights of the strip club across the street splashed garish rainbows across the tall metal racks of clothes. My torch probed around, casting spooky shadows as it lit up diverse articles of period clothing. Stove-pipe hats and spiked Prussian helmets turned into weird distorted giants, and Victorian frock-coats became fluttering black phantoms.

I found a sleeping bag with a portable radio and an ashtray

alongside it. There was a guitar case and underneath the instrument itself was a syringe and a small packet of what I took to be heroin.

I straightened up. To my irritation I found myself unconsciously humming along to one of the banal dirges being played on the juke-box next door. I moved on.

Toorey was just around the end of the rack. In the Party Hire department. She was lying across a fallen harlequin, her broken body clutching him in a bizarre embrace. I didn't have to go any closer to know she had been beaten to death like Pete.

I felt sick, tired and sad. Pete, Toorey, and Charley – I had failed to find any of them. Skindle had rightly been derisive of my powers of deduction. I cheered myself with the thought that he couldn't have held Bill and Roy in very high regard either. Not if he was using all of us to find the stuff for him. It wouldn't surprise me to learn that there were dozens of us out there somewhere.

Some boxes fell over on the floor above. It could have been just a cat. But somehow I knew it wasn't. I started for the door, only to find my feet heading towards the stairs leading above. More boxes fell. I found myself humming along with the juke-box again.

I had switched my torch off and when I got to the top of the stairs, I stood in the semi-darkness, trying to feel a source of human energy. When I thought I had pinpointed it, I suddenly switched on the torch beam. It was a miss. But close. Close enough to make a figure step back into the shadows.

'Ruth?' I called out. 'I found Toorey. Just like I found Pete. I don't know how the Friends of the Inner Light feel about it, but as a sort of Buddhist I can't go along with killing. Not even if you're helping an earwig hurry along to being born into a higher existence.'

There was a rustle of movement in the darkness.

'I've got the photographs,' I went on. 'You can have them. For nothing. I'm not in the blackmail business. Ruth?'

She stepped out into the beam of my torch. There were a pair of nuchakas in her hand. There was blood smeared over them.

'Linda,' I said surprised.

'Where are the photographs?' she demanded.

'Don't tell me you're going into the blackmail business.'

'Don't be ridiculous,' she snapped. 'I love Ruth. And Brian. I don't usually like men that much. But there's something gentle about Brian. It's ironic that he should be the one to start it all.'

'By knocking Ruth up just before he'd decided he was as bent as a two bob watch?' I asked, not feeling especially charitable towards Paxton.

'By telling Toorey that Ruth Armstrong might be her mother. Brian can be a little waspish sometimes. He thought it was a shade hypocritical that a spiritual leader had abandoned her illegitimate child and left her to be brought up in care. Especially when the spiritual leader advocated celibacy as a way to spiritual progress.'

'You can see his point.'

'People change,' she said. 'Nothing in nature is permanent. Are you the same person you were thirty or so years ago?'

I made a small movement, and the nuchakas in her hand swung warningly.

'I bet you're pretty good with those,' I said.

'I am. I spend a lot of time alone. I fill it up with self-improvement. I crocheted rugs before I took up self-defence. Where are the photographs?'

'Not here. Not on me. So it would be pointless coming at me with those things.'

Linda started walking towards me, slowly. The nuchakas picked up the colours from the flashing sign of the strip club across the road.

'Ruth is a very good person now,' she said.

I slid a foot behind me, testing the edge of the stairs.

'How would she feel about you going around battering people to death?' I asked.

'She wouldn't approve. But it had to be done. I couldn't allow her teachings to be destroyed by scandal. Her teachings come from the Source. The Source is greater than any of us. It is important for mankind that the Inner Light is spread. Nothing can be allowed to stop that.'

She stopped and stood facing me, at the end of a long bench.

'Would you mind taking the beam out of my eyes, please?' she asked. 'Thanks. Toorey and Pete were very evil, you know.'

She went on to tell me about them, as the strip-club lighting turned her various shades of garish colour.

Toorey had been taken enough with Brian Paxton's story to go along to St Catherine's House in Aldwych and find a copy of her birth-certificate. She took it along to Ruth Armstrong who accepted her immediately and was more than anxious to make spiritual recompense. But Toorey had been hoping for a more material gesture. She had a habit. And dealers are very down-to-earth people.

On one of the visits to her long lost mother, Toorey met Pete, who was the handyman and resident closet-junkie. Toorey had ended up in his room with a needle in her arm and Pete threshing around on top of her. She had enjoyed the experience, especially because it was taking place with her pious mother meditating a couple of floors below. And it became a regular occurrence.

Toorey had nothing but hatred for the mother who had abandoned her, and she felt she was owed money by her. A lot of money. As payment for the normal childhood that had been taken away from her. When Pete, in a flight of drugged sexual fantasy, had suggested he wouldn't mind giving Ruth one, it had given Toorey an idea for collecting the money she felt she was due.

How they had lured Ruth along to Paxton's office, Linda wasn't sure. But get her along there, they had. It had been over a weekend, when no one was around. They had loaded Ruth's tea with a heavy dose of Valium, set up the camera and the lights. And Pete had fulfilled one of his sexual fantasies.

'How did you find out about it?' I asked.

I thought I heard a noise from down below, but I wasn't sure. It was hard to tell with the racket coming from next door.

'I found Ruth crying one day. In her room. She'd just got the photographs through the post, along with a demand for five thousand pounds. She was totally blown apart. Toorey made no secret about who was doing the blackmailing. She was a very spiteful, hateful person.'

'But she wrote such nice songs.' I said.

'That doesn't mean anything,' Linda said, cynically.

'No,' I agreed, thinking of the long list of creators of

beautiful things who had been moral monsters. 'But it ought to.'

'It used to,' she said. 'Back in the Sixties. People who did nice things, were nice then. But everything changed. Ruth told me the whole story,' she continued. 'I made her promise not to tell anyone else. I promised her I'd get the photographs back and we would burn them together.'

She had worked out that Pete could be hiding in the island house that belonged to the Friends of the Inner Light. She had gone there and attracted his attention by waving from the bank opposite. Pete rowed across eventually, physically confident of being able to handle a woman. Linda told him she had to fetch something from the house. Pete rowed her back across, fairly out of it on something or other.

Once they got into the house, Linda started questioning Pete about the photographs. He had been befuddled enough to suppose she was asking about the Charley at first. He let slip that he and Toorey had panicked, when they heard some detective sergeant was making enquiries about them (an ex-detective sergeant, I was fairly certain).

He and Toorey had split up to make themselves harder to trace. At first he had thought Linda was going to help him.

'He thought he had the physical advantage, because he was a man,' she said contemptuously.

She laughed. It was a thin, high sound that had the back hairs of my neck standing on end.

'I didn't mean to kill him at first,' she said. 'Just give him a good hiding. But I got carried away, thinking of what he had done to Ruth. All those filthy things. In the end I enjoyed it. I felt like an avenging angel. An instrument of justice.'

I thought I heard a foot tread on the wooden stairs below. But I didn't dare take my eyes off Linda. I hoped no one was going to hit me over the head again.

'I was still on the island when you came,' she said.

'It was you who hit me. The nuchakas?'

She shook her head.

'No. I used a tree stump I found. I could get more swing. After all, there was no need to kill you. Not then, anyway.'

'What happened when Toorey showed up?'

'I didn't want to panic her before I got the photographs. I invented some story about having a buyer for the coke they had. I told her Pete had gone to see someone who might be able to help with a really safe place where they could hide out together. Somewhere abroad. I don't think she believed me really. But the thought of even more money made her come back over the river to my car. She was stoned on something as well. I thought she was going to fall into the river a couple of times on the way back.'

I was certain there was someone coming up behind me now. But I still didn't take my eyes off Linda.

'I was tired by then. Exhausted.' She gave another scary laugh. 'After all, I'd never killed anybody before.'

'Absolutely knackering I'm told.'

I was certain I could feel a wave of human energy behind me.

'I dropped her off here. And told her I would come along with a buyer for her coke tonight.'

'Poor Toorey,' I sighed.

'Poor Toorey my arse. She was a nasty, vicious cow. It was she who set those blokes at the Happy Mason onto you. She'd left word for them to have a go at anyone who came round asking questions about her. Paid them money. She told me.'

'Oh well. No point in holding it against her now.'

'I enjoyed killing Toorey,' she said. 'More than Pete, even. I hated her. I think I always did. She was evil. I don't believe Brian was her father.'

'But I was,' said a voice behind me.

Brian Paxton stepped around me and shot Linda three times with the gun he held in his hand.

When I was certain he wasn't going to shoot me as well, I ran over to Linda. She was dying fast. Her boiler suit was soaked through with spurting blood. There was nothing I could do for her now. Nothing anyone could do for her. Except say a prayer maybe. I would leave that to Ruth Armstrong, I decided.

'Brian?' she reached for my hand and I let her take it.

Her eyes stared at me, seeing nothing. Paxton made no move to come closer.

'Brian?' She clutched my hand tighter. 'I'm sorry. I didn't want to hurt you. Not you or Ruth. I loved you both. Why couldn't I have been your daughter?'

'Maybe next time around,' I said. 'Maybe it will work out next time around.'

Her eyelids fluttered like moths banging against a summer evening's window, then stopped. She wasn't breathing any longer.

I laid her down gently, then stood up. Brian Paxton watched me, the gun hanging down by his side.

'It used to belong to The Great Enigmo,' he said, showing me the gun.

'Go on –'

'He was a magician. The highlight of his act was catching live bullets in his teeth. He got it wrong one night.'

'I suppose you'd only have to get it wrong once,' I said.

'Yes. He didn't have any relatives, and I ended up with all his costumes and props. I let the doves go from the top of Parliament Hill Fields.'

'That was nice of you. Linda said you were a gentle sort of man.'

'Why don't you go?' Paxton suggested. 'I'll deal with all this. No reason why you should be involved.'

'No. I suppose not. Will you be alright?'

'Fine,' he assured me.

'Okay then.' I started for the stairs.

'I was Toorey's father,' he said. 'I just knew. Inside somewhere. You can tell about things like that. I loved her. And Linda killed her.'

'Linda loved you. And Ruth. She would have liked you to be her parents.'

'Linda?' he said, surprised. 'I would never have had a daughter like Linda. She was such a frump. Destined to be someone's aunt.'

'Love doesn't have a lot to recommend it sometimes,' I said.

I was walking up the alley, away from the building, when I heard the shot.

Thirty-two

I got up late the next morning. There was a hangover pounding gently on my temples. The soft, but insistent rapping was punishment for the temporary lapse that had taken me into a late night grocery to purchase a couple of bottles of white wine. Somehow, I had managed to stay away from the spirits section. I was glad about that.

On my way back from the health food store, I called in at the newsagent's and picked up an early edition of the midday *Standard*. There was a story about a shoot-out that had taken place over a drugs deal in Soho the previous night. A man and two women had been slain. The police had recovered ten kilos of cocaine and twelve pounds of hash, the story said.

There was a letter lying on my doormat. I picked it up and was puzzling over the postmark when my phone rang. It was Skindle. He wasn't too pleased with what I had to tell him. He agreed that his former comrades at the Met were possibly overdoing it by adding nine kilos of coke and twelve pounds of hash to their find. He suspected promotion-seeking on somebody's part.

Skindle threatened me a few times. But in the end he realised it was pointless, and rang off when he had run out of things to call me.

When I had replaced the receiver, I picked up the letter with the Dumfries postmark. It was from Anita. An attack of conscience had prompted her to send me a postal order for £300.

Thinking I could afford to spend some of the money on paints, I went into the room I use as a studio. Taking a canvas from a pile stacked against the wall, I placed it on my easel. The painting had gone stale on me a few weeks before. For no other reason than the one that has me speeding through France down to Provence, no matter how much I have promised myself a leisurely drive, I was suddenly in a hurry to finish it. An attitude totally opposed to the spirit of the Tao.

Looking at the painting now I saw not an ending, but several possible beginnings. Suggestions for new directions to take. When I came back from posting off the photographs and negatives to Ruth Armstrong, I would have another go at the painting, I thought.